# crêpes wraps
# and ROLLS

# crêpes wraps and ROLLS

## Liz Franklin

PAVILION

For the four men in my life, Chris, Oliver, Tim and David
For munching so happily through the flips and the flops

With all the love in the world xxxx

First published in Great Britain in 2000 by
PAVILION BOOKS LIMITED
London House, Great Eastern Wharf
Parkgate Road, London SW11 4NQ

Text © Liz Franklin 2000
Design and layout © Pavilion Books Ltd

Photography by Ian Wallace 2000

Designed by Isobel Gillan

A CIP catalogue record for this book is available from the British Library.

ISBN 1 86205 4614

Set in Rotis
Printed in Singapore by Tien Wah Press

2 4 6 8 10 9 7 5 3 1

This book can be ordered direct from the publisher. Please contact
the Marketing Department. But try your bookshop first.

# contents

# introduction

Crêpes and pancakes make fabulous food at any time of the day. In this book I would like to share with you a stash of mouthwatering recipes that will show you just how easy it is to prepare them at home. From sophisticated crêpes to simple pancakes and cool tortillas, *Crêpes, Wraps and Rolls* is brimming with ideas and inspiration from all around the world.

Whether stacked and slathered, piled high and poured over, *flambéd*, folded, or wrapped and rolled, crêpes and pancakes are perfect for a savoury feast or a sweet indulgence. They are fun to flip for breakfasts and leisurely brunches, wonderful for stylish suppers and sophisticated enough for the most elegant of dinner parties.

In England, Shrove Tuesday has become synonymous with pancakes. Every year pans are polished, batters are beaten, pancakes are tossed and lemons are squeezed. There are flips *and* flops, but great fun is always had by all! On the same day in French homes crêpes are served to celebrate family life and kindle hopes for happiness and good fortune in the coming years. It is customary to hold a coin in one hand, touch the handle of the frying pan, and make a wish as the pancake is turned.

In fact, pancakes feature in some form or other in almost every culture and country of the world, often as basic street food. Freshly cooked crêpes are sold from little booths on Parisian pavements, they come smothered with jams or purées and nestling in greaseproof wrappers. Under the warm Mediterranean sun Niçoise street vendors scoop sizzling pleats of *La Socca* into paper cones for tourists and locals alike.

Dining out in a typical Breton *crêperie*, you are likely to find delicious *galettes de sarrasin*, dark, buckwheat-speckled pancakes, washed down Breton style with bowls of cool apple cider. The Dutch counterpart is the *pannekoekenhuis*, a distinctive popular restaurant serving not just huge *pannekoeken*, but tiny *poffertjes* as well – the opposite extreme in scale but decidedly moreish!

In Russia the celebrated *blini* comes lavishly topped with fresh caviar and soured cream, and while Italians are passionate about *crespelle*, the Hungarians feel the same way about *palacsinta*. From crisp Jewish *blintzes* and syrup-drenched flapjacks to the flour tortillas that now act as chic and trendy sandwiches, pancakes of every kind are universally adored.

The recipes within these pages combine the traditional and contemporary. While in some cases I have gently tweaked the classics to adapt them for today's busy lifestyles, for the most part they are new, original and exciting. You will discover how straightforward it is to make speedy *blinis*, or delicious Chinese Spring Rolls with Quick Crispy Duck. If you want to provide a delicious lunch for friends, cast off any inhibitions and encase Honey and Tamarind Chicken in warm Sesame Wraps, or take pleasure in a simple supper based around rich Italian flavours with Crêpes *Napolitana*.

For an elegant dessert, consider Coconut Lace Rolls with Troipical Fruit Salsa or Tutti Frutti Blintzes with Blackcurrant Sauce. Want to rustle up a relaxed breakfast? Why not chew over Banana and Pecan Stacks with Maple Butter? Or simply gather around the kitchen table and share traditional crêpes splashed with lemon and sugar.

## Equipment

There are fancy gadgets you *could* use to follow these recipes, from free-standing electric griddles to the ornate stove-top kind. There are pans of all sizes in cast iron and black iron, large skillets and tiny *blini* pans. As a busy mum, when I find a favourite tool to do a certain job – I stick with it. I have a 25 cm/10 in non-stick crêpe pan with shallow sides, and find it invaluable. I used this pan for the majority of recipes in this book. For wraps I sometimes use a slightly larger cast-iron crêpe pan, but my faithful non-stick version is almost as effective. Cast-iron and black-iron pans are brilliant, but before using them for the first time they must be seasoned with salt and oil, heated until smoking, then cooled down and wiped clean. Once this has been done, the pan should merely be wiped after use, never washed. But cast iron is heavy, and for crêpes and pancakes, it helps to use a pan that you can swirl and twirl around easily and comfortably to distribute the batter thinly and evenly across the base.

For flipping I use an old, much-loved palette knife that my mum gave to me many moons ago. Although it now has a tired wooden handle, it remains totally reliable and I can gently loosen the edges of the crêpes before turning them over. It works well for the smaller pancakes and griddle cakes, too.

To make the batter, I use a food processor and for the actual job of swirling the mixture into the pan, I find a small ladle (about 50 ml/2 fl oz/2 tbsp) is very useful, although pouring the batter from a jug works well, too.

A *poffertje* pan is specially designed to make the mini *poffertjes* pancakes from Holland. It is rather like a heavy-based frying pan that has been beaten all over with a hammer to produce small round indentations that are just the right size to mould the pancakes and create the typical curved top. An ordinary griddle or crêpe pan works almost as well – the finished appearance will be slightly different but the taste will be the same.

I would recommend an ice cream machine as one kitchen gadget really worth having, but if you don't have one just turn the mixture into a deep plastic bowl and place it in the freezer. When the mixture is almost frozen, remove and beat it until smooth then return to the freezer until ready to serve. The ice cream won't have the same smooth, silky texture as that churned in a machine, but it should still be delicious.

## For the best results

Try to prepare crêpe batter at least an hour in advance – longer if you can possibly manage it. The standing time will relax the gluten in the flour, and your crêpes will be all the better for it. The batter should be the consistency of pouring cream. Don't be afraid to adjust the amount of liquid or flour if necessary – flours often vary in the exact amount of liquid they absorb.

Crêpes freeze well – simply stack them between layers of greaseproof paper or baking parchment and freeze for up to a month. When you separate them they should defrost in a matter of minutes and they can then be reheated in the oven at 200°C/400°F/Gas 6 for 5–10 minutes. Griddle cakes, however, are best cooked and eaten straight away to enjoy them at their lightest and fluffiest.

So there you have it – now go forth and flip! I wish you good fun and great food!

# larder basics

A larder built upon good foundations will always reflect in your cooking. It's much better to use a small amount of a high quality ingredient than to be generous with something second-rate. For great crêpes and pancakes, here are the basic items I like to keep at hand.

## Baking powder and bicarbonate of soda

Invaluable as raising agents for small pancakes and griddle cakes.

## Butter

Good-quality butter will enhance your cooking – margarine will ruin it.

## Cheese

Parmesan cheese is fabulous for freshly made pesto and other delicious fillings and toppings for crêpes and pancakes. Buy it in blocks and grate as needed. Ricotta cheese makes a perfect stuffing for *crespelle* (Italian crêpes) and featherlight griddlecakes. Mascarpone is wonderfully creamy and versatile, too.

## Cocoa powder

Use pure, dark cocoa powder for baking and dusting.

## Eggs

Buy organic, free-range eggs rather than battery-produced if possible, the flavour is superior and the hens' natural diet significantly reduces the risk of salmonella.

## Flour

Both plain (all-purpose) and self-raising (self-rising) flour are vital for crêpes and pancakes, but I also like to keep a small bag of chickpea flour for making *La Socca* (see page 19) for TV snacks or pre-supper nibbles!

## Garlic

Crucial! For adding flavour to a wide variety of savoury dishes.

## Herbs

Fresh herbs can make such a difference to a variety of sweet and savoury dishes. They have a much better flavour and texture than dried herbs (with the exception of bay leaves), and a garnish of fresh herbs can make even the simplest dish sensational. If you don't have herbs in your garden, why not grow little pots on the kitchen windowsill or outside your kitchen door? My favourites are basil, bay, chives, coriander, mint, parsley, rosemary and thyme.

### Lemons (fresh and preserved)

Fresh lemons are key ingredients for seasoning in my kitchen. When a recipe calls for the zest, try to use organic, unwaxed lemons – they have a nicer flavour.

Tangy preserved lemons are invaluable, too, for adding a burst of concentrated lemon flavour to a recipe. They are easy to make at home. Quarter fresh lemons, leaving them intact at the base. Pack a tablespoonful of coarse sea salt inside each lemon and squash into tall airtight (Kilner) jars. Leave for 3-4 weeks before using, turning the jar occasionally. The salt and juice develop into lemony brine and the peel becomes tender. Top up the jar with extra lemon juice and olive oil.

### Milk

I always use fresh full-fat milk.

### Mustard

Dijon and wholegrain mustards add a delicious kick to fillings, toppings, batters and dough.

### Oils

Extra virgin olive oil is invaluable in the kitchen. I like to keep small quantities infused with herbs, chillies or roasted peppers. Occasionally I will use sunflower oil for frying or preparing mayonnaise.

### Olives

For making tapenade (a tasty dip) and adding great flavour to batters, fillings and dressings – good for nibbling, too!

### Pine nuts

Essential for pesto and lovely with ricotta cheese as a filling for crêpes and *crespelle.*

### Salt

I always use natural sea salt: flakes for sprinkling, coarse for grinding.

### Spices

Wherever possible, buy spices whole and grind them just before using. Among the most useful are whole black peppercorns, dried chillies, cinnamon sticks, coriander seeds, cumin seeds, fennel seeds, ground ginger, whole nutmeg and star anise.

### Tomatoes (tinned and sun-dried)

Tinned chopped tomatoes are invaluable for making sauces. Good-quality sun-dried tomatoes in olive oil are wonderful for flavouring batters and dough, enriching sauces, and adding to roasted vegetables.

Better still are home-dried tomatoes! Slice firm but ripe tomatoes in half lengthways and lay them cut side up on a large roasting tray. Sprinkle with a pinch of sugar, some salt flakes and a grinding of black pepper. Scatter over a little fresh thyme, add a drizzle of olive oil and leave overnight in a low oven 140°C/275°F/Gas 1). If you're not tempted to eat the lot for breakfast the following day – store them in clean airtight jars, covered in olive oil.

## Vinegars

Red wine and white wine vinegars are super for dressings and splashing into sauces. Good balsamic vinegar is worth its weight in gold, and if you can add some fruit vinegars, such as raspberry or mulberry, then all the better.

## Yoghurt

Greek yoghurt is fabulous with crêpes, stirred through with chopped herbs or fruit purée, and makes a lovely alternative to cream with desserts.

## Fruit Conserves and Jams

Good quality fruit conserves and jams make a simple but delicious standby to fill crepes and pancakes. Try to choose those with a fruit content of at least 60% if possible. For a fabulous, quick fruity sauce, simply heat some good quality jam or conserve with a little water, stir until smooth and serve at once!

## Honey

Honey is always a versatile thing to have in any store cupboard, but is especially good trickled over hot pancakes with a dollop of chilled Greek yoghurt.

## Maple Syrup

There's no denying that a good trickle of maple syrup over pancakes can be heavenly but do make sure to buy the real McCoy! Pure maple syrup is expensive but far superior to the nasty imitations that are nothing more than sickly sweet syrups with artificial flavourings.

## Golden Syrup

Often a great favourite with children but not with dentists.

# crêpes

Crêpes and pancakes are so versatile: they offer endless ideas for mealtimes at any time of day, from morning until night. Whether savoury or sweet, from the humblest griddlecake to the grandest crêpe, they can form the basis of a filling breakfast, are brilliant for a quick and simple supper, and can easily take the starring role at an elegant dinner party.

# basic savoury crêpes

French crêpes are famous the world over, and if you visit France you will find that different regions have their own specialities. In the relaxed setting of pancake restaurants (*crêperies*) you can choose from a multitude of savoury and sweet crêpes and enjoy them as an entrée, a main course and – if you have any room left – for dessert as well!

The following basic recipe can be used with a host of savoury toppings and fillings, but for a really special touch try flavouring the batter with finely chopped herbs, spices, or tiny dice of sweet red peppers or crisp spring onions.

If you want to keep the crêpes warm so that you can serve them all together, stack the pancakes between layers of greaseproof paper, cover them loosely with foil and place them on a baking tray in the oven, at 170°C/325°F/Gas 3.

MAKES ABOUT 8 CRÊPES
2 eggs
300 ml/10 fl oz/1½ cups milk
25 g/1 oz/2 tbsp butter, melted
pinch salt

115 g/4 oz/1 cup plain (all purpose) flour, sieved

25 g/1 oz/2 tbsp butter for frying

To make the crêpes, place the eggs, milk and melted butter in a food processor or blender. Whiz to combine. Mix the salt and the flour, add it to the egg mixture and whiz again until you have a smooth batter. Set aside for 30 minutes to an hour, longer if possible.

Lightly butter a non-stick frying pan or crêpe pan and heat over a medium-high heat until hot. If the batter has thickened, it may be necessary to add a little water. Pour in a small amount of batter (about 4 tablespoonfuls, depending on the size of your pan), tilting the pan to spread the mixture over the entire base. Add a little more batter if you have any holes. Cook for 1–2 minutes until the pancake is golden on the underside and bubbles have started to appear on the surface. Using a palette knife, gently loosen the pancake around the edges and flip it over. Cook for another minute until golden brown. Serve immediately or keep warm until ready to serve.

## try another flavour

*Add any of the following to the basic batter mix:*

Black Olive Crêpes: pitted black olives, 10–12 very finely chopped

Cracked Pepper Crêpes: 1 tsp freshly cracked black pepper

Sun-dried Tomato and Basil Crêpes: Add 8 sun-dried tomatoes to the batter in the food processor and whiz to chop the tomatoes finely. Stir in 8–10 torn leaves fresh basil

Poppy Seed Crêpes: 1 tbsp poppy seeds

Herb and Wholegrain Mustard Crêpes: Add 2 tbsp finely chopped chives and 1 tbsp wholegrain mustard

# speedy *blinis*
## with smoked eel and lemon horseradish cream

SERVES 4

### for the *blinis*

65 g/2½ oz/9 tbsp buckwheat
  flour, sieved
40 g/1½ oz/⅓ cup self-raising
  (self-rising) flour, sieved
1 tsp baking powder
salt and freshly ground
  black pepper
1 egg, separated
150 ml/5 fl oz/⅔ cup milk

### for the cream

150 ml/5 fl oz/¼ cup
  crème fraîche
1 tbsp creamed horseradish
zest ½ lemon
2 tsp fresh chives, chopped

### for the topping

115 g/4 oz smoked eel fillet
squeeze lemon juice

25 g/1 oz/2 tbsp butter
  for frying
fresh dill to garnish

Traditional Russian *blinis* are made with a yeast batter but this quick and light variation is a good substitute. Smoked eel is a rather unusual alternative to the customary topping of caviar, and is more affordable, too. Don't worry about having a special *blini* pan – just drop spoonfuls of the mixture on to a hot griddle or use your usual crêpe pan.

To make the *blinis*, place the flours and the baking powder in a large bowl and add a pinch of salt and a good grind of black pepper. Beat the egg yolk and milk together and add this to the flours. Whisk the egg white until stiff, then fold it into the pancake mixture.

Heat a heavy-based pan or griddle and brush lightly with melted butter. Place generous tablespoonfuls of the mixture in the pan, leaving a little space in between each, and cook for 2–3 minutes, until bubbles appear on the surface of each *blini*. Carefully flip the *blinis* over and cook the other sides for a minute or so until golden brown. Repeat with the rest of the mixture.

For the cream, mix the crème fraîche, creamed horseradish, lemon zest and chopped chives together. Chill until needed.

To serve, top the Speedy *Blinis* with a little Horseradish Cream, a piece of smoked eel and a squeeze of lemon juice. Garnish with a grind of black pepper and a sprig of fresh dill and serve immediately.

# buckwheat *galettes*
## with ham and cheese

Buckwheat *galettes* are dark crêpes, speckled with the tiny black flecks that are a characteristic of buckwheat flour. Filled with country ham and topped with a grating of cheese, they make a tasty supper.

SERVES 4

### for the *galettes*

2 eggs

300 ml/10 fl oz/1¼ cups milk

40 g/1½ oz/3 tbsp butter, melted

50 g/2 oz/½ cup plain (all-purpose) flour, sieved

50 g/2 oz/½ cup buckwheat flour, sieved

pinch salt

### for the filling

8 slices country ham

200 g/7 oz/1¾ cups Gruyère or Emmental cheese, grated

2 tsp fresh chives, finely chopped

25 g/1 oz/2 tbsp butter for frying

Preheat the oven to 170°C/325°F/Gas 3.

To make the *galettes*, place the eggs, milk and butter in a food processor and whiz until well mixed. Mix the 2 flours with the salt, add to the egg mixture and whiz until you have a smooth batter. Set aside for at least 30 minutes.

To cook the *galettes*, butter a non-stick frying pan and heat over a medium–high heat until hot. Pour in a small amount of batter (about 4 tablespoonfuls or so, depending on the size of your pan), tilting the pan to spread the mixture over the base. Cook for a minute or so until the pancake is golden on the underside. Gently loosen the pancake around the edges and turn it over to cook the underside for a minute or so longer. Once cooked, stack the crepes between greaseproof paper, cover them with foil and keep warm in the oven until you are ready to use them.

Lay a pancake out flat and place 2 slices of ham in the centre. Fold the 2 opposite sides towards the centre of the crêpe and then fold the top and bottom in too, leaving a central area of ham exposed. Sprinkle with grated cheese and grill for 1–2 minutes, until the cheese is melted and bubbling.

To serve, sprinkle each *galette* with chopped chives and serve immediately.

# la socca

In Nice, *La Socca* are served as street food, cooked and scooped into cones of greaseproof paper and sprinkled with salt or sugar. They are made with chickpea flour and have an intriguing flavour, at first I found it quite bland. My version includes a kick of cracked peppercorns and pungent fennel seeds. Try them hot, fresh from the pan, or grilled until crisp, sprinkled with salt and served as a nibble with pre-dinner drinks.

SERVES 4-6

130 g/4½ oz chickpea flour

1 tsp salt

1 tbsp cracked, mixed peppercorns

1 generous tsp fennel seeds

200 ml/7 fl oz/scant 1 cup water

4 tbsp olive oil for frying

sea salt to sprinkle

To make the *La Socca*, place the chickpea flour, salt, cracked peppercorns and fennel seeds in a food processor or blender. Whiz until everything is well mixed. With the motor running, add enough water to produce a thin, smooth batter. Set aside for 30 minutes or so.

To cook the *La Socca*, put a little olive oil into a non-stick frying pan or crêpe pan. When the pan is fairly hot, pour in a small amount of batter (about 50 ml/ 2 fl oz/¼ cup, depending on the size of your pan). Tilt the pan to spread the mixture over the entire base. Cook for 1-2 minutes, until the crêpe is golden on the underside and bubbles have started to appear on the surface. Using a palette knife, gently loosen the crêpe around the edges and turn it over to cook the underside for 20-30 seconds.

Turn the crêpe out and serve immediately sprinkled with a little sea salt.

Alternatively, for a great nibble to go with pre-dinner drinks, sprinkle with a little sea salt and place under the grill to crisp up. Remove and snap pieces off to eat while still warm.

# herb and mustard crêpe purses
## with dill and lemon prawns

These tasty crêpes are stuffed with fresh prawns tossed in a lemon and dill mayonnaise, and tied to form little moneybags. They make a great summer lunch served with a crisp salad. Extra virgin olive oil tends to make quite a heavy mayonnaise, so I generally use a light olive oil. Sunflower oil or grapeseed oil would also make good substitutes.

SERVES 4

4 Herb and Wholegrain Mustard Crêpes
(see page 15)

### for the mayonnaise

1 egg
zest 2 lemons
juice 1 lemon
1 tsp Dijon mustard

300 ml/10 fl oz/1¼ cups light olive oil
salt and freshly ground black pepper

### for the filling

450 g/1 lb cooked peeled prawns
1 tbsp fresh dill, finely chopped
salt and freshly ground black pepper

4 long lengths of chive to tie the purses

To make the mayonnaise, place the egg, lemon zest, 1 tbsp lemon juice, mustard and a pinch of salt in the bowl of a blender. Whiz to combine. With the motor running, begin to trickle in the olive oil slowly until you have added about a third, then add the remaining oil more quickly. When all the oil has been incorporated, add the remaining lemon juice and adjust the seasoning, adding a little more salt if necessary and a little freshly ground black pepper. Whiz again to blend.

For the filling, mix 150 ml/5 fl oz/⅔ cup mayonnaise with the prawns and stir in the chopped dill. Season to taste. Lay a crêpe out flat and place a quarter of the prawn mixture in the centre. Gather the edges of the crêpe together to form a purse and tie carefully with a long length of chive.

To serve, place a crêpe purse on each of 4 pretty plates and accompany with a mixed salad.

# Ollie's sweetcorn pancakes

These simple, golden sweetcorn pancakes have long been a favourite with us at home. They make a refreshing change served as part of a vegetable selection with a Sunday roast. They're also great for a quick vegetarian lunch or light supper – if you have some sweetcorn in the freezer, a few eggs and a spare onion – you're almost there!

SERVES 4

350 g/12 oz/2 cups sweetcorn, cooked

3 eggs, separated

1 red onion, finely chopped

2 tbsp fresh chives, finely chopped

50 g/2 oz/½ cup self-raising
  (self-rising) flour

salt and freshly ground black pepper

25 g/1 oz/2 tbsp butter for frying

To make the pancakes, place the cooked sweetcorn in a large bowl and stir in the egg yolks. Add the red onion and chives. Stir in the self-raising flour until everything is well mixed. Whisk the egg whites until stiff but not dry, then stir a generous tablespoonful into the pancake mixture to loosen it. Carefully fold in the remaining egg white. Season well with salt and freshly ground black pepper.

Heat a heavy-based pan or griddle and brush lightly with melted butter. Place generous tablespoonfuls of the mixture on the pan, leaving a little space in between each, and cook for 3–4 minutes until bubbles appear on the surface of each pancake. Carefully flip the pancakes over and cook the other side for a further 2–3 minutes until golden brown and firm to the touch. Repeat with the rest of the mixture.

Serve at once, or keep warm in the oven at 170°C/325°F/Gas 3 until you are ready to serve.

# pasta *carbonara* pancakes

Classic Italian pasta *alla carbonara* has long been a favourite supper dish to rustle up at home. The essential ingredient is pancetta, Italian bacon made from cured and lightly spiced pork belly that goes deliciously crisp when fried. One lunchtime I came up with the idea of using mini pasta shapes and turning them into crisp little pancakes. They made a lovely lunch with a big, crunchy salad, and now we have them all the time.

SERVES 4

130 g/4½ oz dried mini pasta shapes

2 tbsp olive oil

1 small onion, finely chopped

1 clove garlic, crushed

90 g/3½ oz pancetta, cubed (or bacon lardons)

3 eggs, separated

50 ml/2fl oz/¼ cup double (heavy) cream

40 g/1½ oz/½ cup Parmesan cheese, grated

salt and freshly ground black pepper

25 g/1 oz/2 tbsp butter for frying

mixed salad and warm crusty bread to serve

To make the pancakes, cook the mini pasta shapes until *al dente*, following the packet instructions. Drain through a colander, rinse with cold water and drain again. Set aside.

Heat a tablespoonful of olive oil in a pan and sauté the onion and garlic until soft but not brown. Turn into a large bowl and stir in the cooked pasta. Sauté the pancetta or lardons in the remaining oil for 3–4 minutes until golden brown and crisp. Drain on kitchen paper.

In the meantime, mix the egg yolks, double cream and Parmesan together. Stir in the cooked pancetta, then add this to the pasta mixture. Stir well. Whisk the egg whites until stiff and stir a couple of tablespoonfuls into the pancake mixture. Carefully fold in the remaining egg whites and season to taste.

Heat a heavy-based pan or griddle and brush lightly with melted butter. Place generous tablespoonfuls of the mixture in the pan, leaving a little space in between each, and cook for 2–3 minutes until bubbles appear on the surface of each pancake. Carefully flip the pancakes over and cook the other side until golden brown. Repeat with the rest of the mixture.

Serve immediately with mixed salad and some warm crusty bread.

# courgette, feta and
## sun-dried tomato pancakes

These little savoury pancakes are full of tasty, crumbly feta – one of my favourite cheeses. Serve them with a crisp salad and plenty of crusty Italian bread. Look out for aromatic fresh green peppercorns in brine in the spice section in major supermarkets.

SERVES 4

### for the pancakes

300 g/11 oz courgettes (zucchini), washed
  and coarsely grated
1 small red onion, finely chopped
12 sun-dried tomatoes, quartered

1 tsp fresh thyme leaves, chopped
½ tsp fresh green peppercorns
2 eggs, separated
75 g/3 oz/²⁄₃ cup plain (all-purpose) flour
250 g/9 oz feta cheese
salt and freshly ground black pepper

25 g/1 oz/2 tbsp butter for frying

Preheat the oven to 170°C/325°F/Gas 3.

To make the pancakes, place the courgettes, red onion, sun-dried tomatoes and thyme in a large bowl and stir well. Crush the peppercorns using a pestle and mortar and add these to the mixture, with the egg yolks. Stir in the flour. Crumble the feta and stir lightly into the mixture. Whisk the egg whites until stiff and stir a generous tablespoonful into the pancake mixture. Carefully fold in the remaining egg white. Season to taste.

Heat a heavy-based pan or griddle and brush lightly with melted butter. Place generous tablespoonfuls of the mixture onto the pan, leaving a little space in between each, and cook for 2–3 minutes, until bubbles appear on the surface of each pancake. Carefully flip the pancakes over and cook the other side for a further 2–3 minutes until golden brown and firm to the touch. Repeat with the rest of the mixture. Place the pancakes on a baking tray and keep warm in the oven until all the pancakes are cooked.

Serve immediately with a crisp salad and some warm crusty bread.

# dutch *poffertjes*

*Poffertjes* are slightly larger than bite-size pancakes and are a popular dish all over Holland. Served with both savoury and sweet toppings, they are cooked in a special *poffertjes* pan (see Equipment page 8) but an ordinary griddle or crêpe pan works almost as well. They are delightful for a relaxed weekend brunch but do try the sweet version on page 60, too.

SERVES 4

### for the *poffertjes*

130 g/4½ oz/1 cup plus 2 tbsp self-raising
  (self-rising) flour, sieved
½ tsp baking powder

pinch salt
1 egg
150 ml/5 fl oz/²⁄₃ cup milk
15 g/½ oz/1 tbsp butter, melted

25 g/1 oz/2 tbsp butter, melted, for frying
crisp bacon and scrambled eggs to serve

To make the *poffertjes*, mix the flour, baking powder and salt together in a large bowl. Whisk together the egg, milk and melted butter and add this to the flour mixture. Stir well.

Heat a *poffertjes* pan, a griddle or heavy-based pan over a medium–high heat and brush lightly with melted butter. If you have a *poffertjes* pan, fill the little holes with batter using a teaspoon. If you are using a griddle or heavy-based pan, place teaspoonfuls of the mixture in the pan, leaving a little space in between each, and cook for 1–2 minutes until bubbles appear on the surface of each *poffertje*. Carefully flip the *poffertjes* over and cook for 2–3 minutes more until firm, risen and golden brown.

Serve immediately or place the cooked pancakes on a baking tray and keep warm in the oven at 170°C/325°F/Gas 3 until required.

Serve the *poffertjes* warm with crispy bacon and scrambled eggs.

# spekpannekoek
## traditional Netherlands
## bacon pancakes

While the French are renowned for their crêpes, the people of the Netherlands are just as passionate about *pannekoeken*. The *Pannekoekenhuis* is a very popular and distinctive type of restaurant found all over Holland and is generally devoted to serving a delicious array of crisp, golden pancakes. This one, packed with bacon, is great as part of a hearty breakfast or leisurely brunch served with piping hot scrambled eggs.

SERVES 4

1 tbsp olive oil

130 g/4½ oz/1 cup bacon lardons (or
   pancetta cubes)

130 g/4½ oz/1 cup plus 2 tbsp self-raising
   (self-rising) flour, sieved

½ tsp baking powder

1 egg

1 tbsp mustard

1 tbsp fresh chives, finely chopped

salt and freshly ground black pepper

4 tbsp sunflower oil for frying

To make the *spekpannekoek*, heat the olive oil in a pan and fry the lardons or pancetta for 3–4 minutes until crisp. Drain on kitchen paper and set aside. Mix the flour and baking powder together in a large bowl and stir in the egg, mustard and chives. Season well with salt and freshly ground black pepper.

Pour the sunflower oil into a frying pan. When it is hot, drop generous tablespoons of the mixture into the pan, leaving a little space in between each. Sprinkle a little of the cooked bacon immediately on to the uncooked surface, so that the bacon will stay crisp and clearly visible when the pancake is cooked. Cook for 2–3 minutes until bubbles appear on the surface of each pancake. Carefully flip the pancakes over and cook the other side for a further minute or so until golden brown. Repeat with the rest of the mixture.

To retain their crispness, it is best to serve the pancakes at once, although they can be kept warm in the oven at 170°C/325°F/Gas 3 for a short time until you are ready to serve.

# peppered crêpe *tagliatelle*
## with feta, tomatoes and olives

Although I love pasta, I must admit that a crisp-fried tangle of pepper spiked crêpes is a terrific alternative to *tagliatelle*. Salty feta cheese and hot, oven baked cherry tomatoes are always a winning combination. Shiny black olives and fresh basil are the icing on the cake! I hope you love this dish as much as I do.

SERVES 4

8 Cracked Pepper Crêpes (see page 15)

### for the topping

450 g/1 lb cherry tomatoes

1 clove garlic, crushed

1 tsp caster (superfine) sugar

1 tbsp balsamic vinegar

2 tbsp olive oil

salt and freshly ground black pepper

200 g/7 oz feta cheese, lightly crumbled

about 20 black olives, pitted

fresh basil and freshly ground black pepper
  to garnish

You will need a deep-fat fryer

Preheat the oven to 220°C/425°F/Gas 7.

First, cut the crêpes into long strips about 1 cm/½ in wide (an easy way to do this is to roll them up and cut them into strips with kitchen scissors). Set aside.

To make the topping, wash the tomatoes and place in an ovenproof dish. Sprinkle with the garlic and sugar. Drizzle over the balsamic vinegar and olive oil. Season with a little salt and freshly ground black pepper. Place in the oven for 8–10 minutes until the skins begin to pop and the juices are released. Remove from the oven and keep warm.

Heat the olive oil in a deep-fat fryer to 190°C/375°F and sauté the strips of crêpe until crisp. Drain quickly on kitchen paper.

To serve, divide the crispy crêpe *tagliatelle* between 4 rustic dinner plates. Scatter with the tomatoes, feta cheese and olives, turning them through very lightly with a fork. Garnish with fresh basil and a grind of black pepper and serve immediately.

# chilli stacks

Serving individual stacks of rice pancakes layered with spicy ground chilli beef make a lovely unusual variation on the popular Mexican dish *chili con carne*.

SERVES 4

## for the pancakes

165 g/5½ oz/½ cup mixed white basmati and wild rice (uncooked weight)
2 small red onions, peeled, cut into halves and finely sliced
2 eggs, separated
2 tbsp fresh chives, finely chopped
40 g/1½ oz/3 tbsp butter, melted
40 g/1½ oz/3 tbsp plain (all-purpose) flour
salt and freshly ground black pepper

## for the filling

2 tbsp olive oil
1 large onion, finely chopped
2 cloves garlic, crushed
2 tbsp cumin seeds, toasted
450 g/1 lb minced beef
1 × 400 g/14 oz/large tin chopped tomatoes
15 sun-dried tomatoes, coarsely chopped
200 ml/7 fl oz/scant 1 cup beef stock
4 tbsp Worcester sauce
1 tbsp paprika
1–2 fresh chillies, deseeded and very finely chopped
1 × 200 g/7 oz/small tin red kidney beans, drained
2 tbsp fresh coriander (cilantro), chopped

## for the topping

150 ml/5 fl oz/⅔ cup soured cream
2 tbsp fresh chives, finely chopped

6 tbsp oil for frying
fresh coriander (cilantro) to garnish

Preheat the oven to 170°C/325°F/Gas 3.

To make the pancakes, cook the rice following the packet instructions. Drain the rice and rinse with cold water. Set aside. Place the sliced red onions, egg yolks and chives in a large bowl and stir. Add the cooled rice and the melted butter. Add the flour and stir well. Whisk the egg whites until stiff, then carefully fold them into the rice mixture. Season well.

Heat a griddle or heavy-based pan and brush lightly with melted butter. Place generous tablespoonfuls of the mixture in the pan, leaving a little space in between each, and flattening them slightly with the back of a spoon. Cook for 2–3 minutes until bubbles appear on the surface of each pancake. Carefully flip the pancakes over and cook the other side for a further 2–3 minutes until golden brown. Repeat with the rest of the mixture.

To keep the pancakes warm until you are ready to use them, lay them on a baking tray, cover them loosely with foil and place in the oven. Alternatively, you can freeze them; simply reheat at 190°C/375°F/Gas 5 for 4 to 5 minutes just before serving.

For the chilli filling, heat the olive oil in a pan and sauté the onion and garlic until soft but not brown. Add the cumin seeds and stir. Add the minced beef and cook until brown. Sieve the chopped tomatoes and refrigerate the juice to use in another recipe. Stir the tomato flesh and sun-dried tomatoes into the beef mixture. Add the stock, Worcester sauce, paprika and chillies. Let the mixture bubble over a low heat for 25–30 minutes. Add the kidney beans and coriander and cook for 2–3 minutes more.

In the meantime, mix the soured cream together with the chives and refrigerate until needed.

To serve, place a rice pancake in the centre of a dinner plate. Spoon some of the chilli mixture on top. Place another pancake on top, followed by some more chilli mixture. Repeat the layering one more time, using a third pancake and ending with a layer of chilli mix. Repeat with the other pancakes. Drizzle the tops with a little of the soured-cream mixture and garnish with a sprig of fresh coriander. Serve immediately.

# crêpes *napolitana*

These crêpes are packed with all the rich tomato flavours of an authentic Italian pizza, but are much quicker to make. I always use cherry tomatoes in preference to the ordinary chopped variety for making tomato sauces. Although they will pop open as they bubble down and release their juices, they still retain a little shape and emerge as shiny blobs to make the sauce look wonderful. Look out for them in major supermarkets, but if you have trouble finding them, ordinary chopped tomatoes will be fine.

SERVES 4

8 Basic Crêpes (see page 14)

handful fresh basil leaves

salt and freshly ground black pepper

### for the filling

2 tbsp olive oil

1 large onion, chopped

2 cloves garlic, crushed

2 × 400 g/14 oz/large tins cherry or chopped
   tomatoes

1 tsp sugar

### for the topping

200 g/7 oz mozzarella cheese, grated

olive oil to drizzle

fresh basil to garnish

mixed salad leaves to serve

To make the tomato filling, heat the olive oil in a pan and sauté the onions and garlic until soft but not coloured. Add the tomatoes and the sugar, and stir. Tear the basil into pieces and add half of them to the pan. Season to taste. Let the sauce bubble over a low heat for about 20 minutes or so until it thickens. Stir in the remaining basil. Check the seasoning and adjust if necessary.

Lay a crêpe out flat on a large ovenproof platter and spread some tomato sauce over 1 quarter. Fold the crêpe in half and in half again to make a fan shape. Repeat with the other crêpes, then place them on a large heatproof plate, sprinkle a little mozzarella cheese on top of each crêpe, grind over a little black pepper and drizzle over a little olive oil. Grill for 2–3 minutes until the cheese is melted and bubbling.

To serve, place 2 crêpes on each dinner plate, garnish with fresh basil and serve immediately with a crisp green salad.

# salmon *crespelle*
## with ginger and wholegrain mustard and watercress sauce

SERVES 4

8 Basic Crêpes (see page 14)

### for the filling

500 g/1¼ lb salmon fillet, skinned and pinboned (use a pair of tweezers to remove the tiny pinbones from the fillets)

1 tbsp lemon juice

3–4 knobs preserved stem ginger, rinsed and chopped

2 tbsp currants

75 g/3 oz/6 tbsp butter, softened

1 tbsp fresh coriander (cilantro), finely chopped

salt and freshly ground black pepper

### for the sauce

90 g/3½ oz fresh watercress

300 ml/10 fl oz/1¼ cups single (light) cream

1 tbsp wholegrain mustard

salt and freshly ground black pepper

1 tbsp butter for the ovenproof dish

1 lemon, cut into 4 wedges, and a little extra watercress to garnish

A *crespelle* is an Italian crêpe, with a tasty filling that is baked in the oven. This is an unusual combination – raw salmon, stem ginger and currants – but the result is perfectly cooked salmon with a fabulous flavour. An easy watercress sauce, spiked with tangy wholegrain mustard, provides the perfect accompaniment.

Preheat the oven to 200°C/400°F/Gas 6.

To make the filling, cut the salmon into 1 cm/½ in cubes and place in a large bowl with the lemon juice. Mix together the stem ginger, currants and softened butter. Work this mixture gently through the salmon chunks, then add the coriander. Season with salt and freshly ground black pepper.

Lightly brush an ovenproof dish with melted butter. Lay a crêpe out flat and spoon an eighth of the mixture on to the centre. Fold into a flat parcel. Repeat with all the crêpes and place them in the prepared dish in a single layer, seam-side down. Cook for 20–25 minutes until the tops of the pancakes are crisp, and the salmon is cooked through but still opaque.

Meanwhile, place the watercress and cream in a food processor or blender and whiz for 1–2 minutes until smooth. Add the mustard and season to taste.

To serve, place 2 Salmon *Crespelle* on each dinner plate. Garnish with a wedge of lemon and a sprig of watercress, then serve immediately with Wholegrain Mustard and Watercress Sauce.

# ricotta and tomato stack

This is a good recipe for late summer, when tomatoes are ripe and tasty. It looks just like a savoury gateau – stacked with fluffy white ricotta cheese and flecked with fresh basil and pine nuts. It needs to be left in the fridge for an hour or so to firm up, to make it easy to cut, and when you slice it, each attractive layer will be clearly visible.

**SERVES 4 AS A MAIN COURSE**
**OR 6–8 AS A STARTER**

6 Sun-dried Tomato and Basil Crêpes (see page 15)

### for the filling

500 g/1¼ lb/2 cups ricotta cheese
4 ripe but firm tomatoes, deseeded and chopped
handful fresh basil, torn into small pieces
50 g/2 oz/½ cup pine nuts, toasted
salt and freshly ground black pepper
2–3 tbsp fresh chives, chopped

salad leaves to garnish

To make the filling, mix the ricotta cheese, tomatoes and the basil together in a large bowl. Add the pine nuts, stir and season well with salt and freshly ground black pepper.

Trim the pancakes until they measure about 15 cm/6 in (I usually cut around a large side plate). Layer the pancakes with the ricotta mixture, taking care to spread the mixture evenly. When the stack is complete, press chopped chives around the edges. Chill for an hour or so until firm.

To serve, cut into slices and garnish with a few dressed salad leaves.

# cheese `n` chive
## potato pancakes

When you're serving side vegetables it's nice to offer an alternative to the usual potatoes, and these cheesy potato pancakes fit the bill perfectly. This is a great recipe to call upon when you haven't had a chance to shop. If you have potatoes and cheese, all you really need is a few extra store cupboard ingredients. They are yummy served with the rich tomato sauce used for Crêpes *Napolitana* on page 33.

SERVES 4

450 g/1 lb potatoes, boiled and mashed

1 clove garlic, crushed

4 spring onions, finely chopped

1 tbsp mustard

2 tbsp fresh chives, finely chopped

75 g/3 oz/³⁄₄ cup extra strong Cheddar cheese, grated

2 eggs, separated

50 g/2 oz/¹⁄₂ cup self-raising (self-rising) flour

1 tsp baking powder

salt and freshly ground black pepper

25 g/1 oz/2 tbsp butter for frying

To make the pancakes, place the mashed potatoes in a large bowl and stir in the garlic, spring onions, mustard and chives. Add the grated cheese and egg yolks. Mix the flour and baking powder together, add this to the mixture and stir until everything is fully incorporated. Whisk the egg whites until stiff, then stir a generous tablespoonful into the pancake mixture to loosen it. Carefully fold in the remaining egg whites. Season with salt and freshly ground black pepper.

Heat a griddle or heavy-based pan and brush lightly with melted butter. Place generous tablespoonfuls of the mixture in the pan, leaving a little space in between each, and cook for 3–4 minutes until golden brown. Carefully flip the pancakes over and cook the other sides for 3–4 minutes. Repeat with the rest of the mixture.

Serve immediately, or place the cooked pancakes on a baking tray and keep warm in the oven at 170°C/325°F/Gas 3 until required.

# crunchy noodle pancakes
## with spicy sherry prawns

These crunchy little pancakes are great to serve cocktail size, with a variety of toppings as pre-dinner nibbles. Children seem to love them too! Make sure you dry the cooked noodles before you add the ground rice and fry them. Drain them well on kitchen paper after cooking and serve them as soon as possible.

SERVES 4

### for the pancakes

75 g/3 oz vermicelli rice noodles
½ tsp ground rice
salt and freshly ground black pepper
50 ml/2 fl oz/¼ cup sunflower oil for frying

### for the prawns

1 tbsp good-quality tomato ketchup
2 tbsp roasted-pepper olive oil
1 tsp sherry
200 g/7 oz cooked tiger prawns, peeled
pinch chilli flakes

paprika and fresh coriander (cilantro)
to garnish

To make the pancakes, soak the noodles in boiling water following the instructions on the packet. Drain well (I give them a good squeeze with plenty of kitchen paper). Add the ground rice, season and stir. Pour the oil into a frying pan and when it is hot (but not smoking) place tablespoonfuls of the mixture in the pan, pressing them with the back of a spoon to make very flat circular pancakes. Cook for 3-4 minutes until crisp and golden.

To retain their crispness, it is best to serve the pancakes immediately, although they can be kept warm in the oven at 170°C/325°F/Gas 3 for a short time until you are ready to serve.

For the prawns, mix the tomato ketchup, pepper oil and sherry together in a small bowl. Stir this into the prawns. Add a pinch of chilli flakes and season to taste.

To serve, top the Crunchy Noodle Pancakes with some Spicy Sherry Prawns, sprinkle with a little paprika and garnish with sprigs of fresh coriander.

# basic sweet crêpes

This batter differs from the Shrove Tuesday pancakes on page 44 in that it contains a small amount of butter and natural vanilla extract to make it slightly richer. The batter can also be flavoured with a little alcohol, which makes the crêpes a touch more sophisticated and a little crisper, too. Choose the alcohol to complement your topping or filling; for instance, crêpes served with apples are delicious with a little Calvados in the batter, or try a dash of rum in a crêpe to partner bananas.

MAKES ABOUT 8 CRÊPES
2 eggs
300 ml/10 fl oz/1¼ cups milk
1 tsp vanilla extract
40 g/1½ oz/3 tbsp butter, melted
40 g/1½ oz/3 tbsp caster (superfine) sugar

pinch salt
130 g/4½ oz/1 cup plus 2 tbsp plain
 (all-purpose) flour, sieved

25 g/1 oz/2 tbsp butter for frying

To make the crêpes, place the eggs, milk, vanilla extract and melted butter in a food processor or blender. Add the sugar and salt and whiz until everything is well mixed. Add the flour and whiz again until you have a smooth batter. Set aside for 30 minutes to an hour, or longer if possible.

Lightly butter a non-stick frying pan or crêpe pan and heat over a medium-high heat until hot. If the batter has thickened, it may be necessary to add a little water. Pour in a small amount of batter (about 4 tablespoonfuls), tilting the pan to spread the mixture over the entire base. Add a little more batter if you have any holes. Cook for 1–2 minutes until the pancake is golden on the underside and bubbles start to appear on the surface of each crêpe. Using a palette knife, gently loosen the pancake around the edges and turn it over. Cook for another minute until golden brown.

Serve immediately, or if you want to keep the crêpes warm so that you can serve them all together, stack the pancakes between layers of greaseproof paper, cover them loosely in foil and place them on a baking tray in the oven at 170°C/325°F/Gas 3.

# blueberry and cream cheese pancakes
## with blueberry sauce

Fresh plump blueberries are a popular ingredient in American flap-jacks, and it is easy to see why. Adding cream cheese and blueberries to these pancakes gives them a really lovely flavour. They make a great breakfast or brunch served with a quick blueberry sauce.

SERVES 4

### for the pancakes

150g/5 oz/²⁄₃ cup cream cheese
pinch salt
50 g/2 oz/¹⁄₄ cup caster (superfine) sugar
25 g/1 oz/2 tbsp butter, melted
3 eggs, separated
4 tbsp milk
1 tsp vanilla extract

115 g/4 oz/1 cup self-raising (self-rising) flour, sieved
150 g/5 oz blueberries

### for the sauce

175 g/6 oz good-quality blueberry conserve
2 tbsp water

25 g/1 oz/2 tbsp butter for frying
icing (confectioner's) sugar to dust

To make the pancakes, beat together the cream cheese, salt, sugar, melted butter, egg yolks, milk and vanilla extract in a large bowl. Fold in the flour.

Whisk the egg whites until stiff and stir a tablespoonful into the pancake mixture. Carefully fold in the remaining egg white. Gently stir in the blueberries.

Heat a griddle or heavy-based pan and brush lightly with melted butter. Place tablespoonfuls of the mixture in the pan, leaving a little space in between each, and cook for 2–3 minutes until bubbles appear on the surface of each pancake. Carefully flip the pancakes over and cook the other side for 2–3 minutes until golden brown.

Serve immediately or place the cooked pancakes on a baking tray and keep warm in the oven at 170°C/325°F/Gas 3 until required.

Meanwhile, gently heat the blueberry conserve and water in a small pan.

Serve the Blueberry and Cream Cheese Pancakes dusted with a little icing sugar and drizzled with warm Blueberry Sauce.

# shrove tuesday pancakes
## for pancake day

Shrove Tuesday heralds the beginning of Lent, and the traditional serving of pancakes came about as a way of using up surplus eggs and fat before the forty-day fast began. In England the day is known as Pancake Day and it is celebrated everywhere in a variety of wacky and wonderful ways.

Each pancake has to be tossed of course, and they can then be smeared with jam or sprinkled with sugar and lemon – and eaten in seconds! For a savoury version, simply omit the caster sugar.

**MAKES ABOUT 8 PANCAKES**
2 eggs
300 ml/10 fl oz/1¼ cups milk
25 g/1 oz/2 tbsp caster (superfine) sugar
pinch salt

115 g/4 oz/1 cup plain (all-purpose) flour, sieved

25 g/1 oz/2 tbsp butter for frying

To make the pancakes, place the eggs and milk into a food processor or blender with the sugar and salt. Whiz until everything is well mixed. Add the flour and whiz again until you have a smooth batter. Set aside for at least 30 minutes, or as long as possible.

Lightly butter a non-stick frying pan or crêpe pan and heat over a medium high heat until hot. If the batter has thickened, it may be necessary to add a little water. Pour in a small amount of batter (about 4 tablespoonfuls depending on the size of your pan), tilting the pan to spread the mixture over the entire base. Add a little more batter if you have any holes. Cook for 1–2 minutes until the pancake is golden on the underside and bubbles start to appear on the surface of each pancake. Using a palette knife, gently loosen the pancake around the edges and turn it over. Cook for another minute until golden brown.

Serve immediately, or if you want to keep the crêpes warm so that you can serve them all together, stack the pancakes between layers of greaseproof paper, cover them loosely in foil and place them on a baking tray in the oven at 170°C/325°F/Gas 3.

# lemon and ricotta pancakes

## with fresh raspberry sauce

SERVES 4

### for the pancakes

250 g/9 oz/scant 1¼ cups
  ricotta cheese
pinch salt
50 g/2 oz/¼ cup caster
  (superfine) sugar
25 g/1 oz/2 tbsp butter, melted
3 eggs, separated
zest 2 lemons
50 g/2 oz/½ cup plain
  (all-purpose) flour, sieved

### for the sauce

250 g/9 oz/1½ cups fresh ripe
  raspberries
2 tbsp Framboise liqueur
50 g/2 oz/¼ cup caster
  (superfine) sugar

25 g/1oz/2 tbsp butter for
  frying
icing (confectioner's) sugar
  to dust
extra raspberries to garnish

Whenever I serve these fluffy pillows of ricotta, they always seem to disappear in seconds. Ricotta cheese is the main ingredient in the pancakes, and combined with a little flour and a mass of billowy, whipped egg white, the result is featherlight and delicate.

To make the pancakes, beat together the ricotta, salt, sugar, melted butter, egg yolks and lemon zest in a large bowl. Fold in the flour. Whisk the egg whites until stiff and stir a tablespoonful into the pancake mixture. Carefully fold in the remaining egg white.

Heat a griddle or heavy-based pan and brush lightly with melted butter. Place tablespoonfuls of the mixture in the pan, leaving a little space in between each, and cook for 2–3 minutes until bubbles appear on the surface of each pancake. Carefully flip the pancakes over and cook the other sides for a further 2–3 minutes until golden brown.

Serve immediately or place the cooked pancakes on a baking tray and keep warm in the oven at 170°C/325°F/Gas 3 until required.

For the sauce, place the raspberries in a blender or food processor and purée, then sieve to remove the seeds. Add the Framboise liqueur and sweeten the purée with caster sugar. The exact amount of sugar will vary according to how ripe the fruit is.

Serve the warm Lemon and Ricotta Pancakes with the Fresh Raspberry Sauce, dust with icing sugar and garnish with a few fresh raspberries.

# fizzy orange crêpes
## with peach and cardamom butter

It's the sparkling mineral water added to the batter that makes these crêpes beautifully crisp and light. Flavoured butters, both sweet and savoury, play quite a big part in my kitchen. They can give such a lift to all manner of things – even a humble slice of toast! You can find dried peaches in most large supermarkets, and when you add them to fresh butter with finely crushed seeds of fragrant cardamom, the result is a perfumed butter with a delightful flavour.

SERVES 4

### for the crêpes

2 eggs

zest 2 oranges

200 ml/7 fl oz/scant 1 cup sparkling mineral water

7 tbsp milk

40 g/1½ oz/3 tbsp caster (superfine) sugar

115 g/4 oz/1 cup plain (all-purpose) flour, sieved

pinch salt

### for the butter

150 g/5 oz/1¼ sticks butter, softened

200 g/7 oz ready-to-eat dried peaches

2 cardamom pods

2 tbsp caster (superfine) sugar

25 g/1 oz/2 tbsp butter for frying

mint leaves to garnish

icing (confectioner's) sugar to dust

       *continued overleaf*

To make the crêpes, place the eggs, orange zest, fizzy water and milk in the bowl of a food processor or blender and whiz. Add the sugar and the flour and whiz again until you have a smooth batter. Set aside for 30 minutes to an hour, longer if possible.

For the peach and cardamom butter, place the softened butter and dried peaches in a food processor. Remove the tiny black seeds from the cardamom pods (you should get about 8 seeds) and crush with a pestle and mortar. Add the seeds to the butter and peaches with the sugar. Whiz everything together until the peaches are fully incorporated and you have a smooth butter. Turn the mixture into a clean bowl and refrigerate until required.

When you are ready to cook the crêpes, lightly butter a non-stick frying pan or crêpe pan and heat over a medium high heat until hot. If the batter has thickened, it may be necessary to add a little water. Pour in a small amount of batter (about 4 tablespoonfuls, depending on the size of your pan), tilting the pan to spread the mixture over the entire base. Add a little more batter if you have any holes. Cook for 1–2 minutes until the pancake is golden on the underside and bubbles start to appear on the surface of each crêpe. Using a palette knife, gently loosen the pancake around the edges, turn it over and cook for a further minute until golden.

If you want to keep the crêpes warm so that you can serve them all together, stack the pancakes between layers of greaseproof paper, cover them loosely in foil and place them on a baking tray in the oven at 170°C/325°F/Gas 3.

To serve, fold the crêpes into quarters to create fan shapes, add a generous dollop of Peach and Cardamom Butter and garnish with a little fresh mint. Add a dusting of icing sugar if you wish.

# banana and pecan stacks
## with maple butter

Sweet, ripe bananas contrast beautifully with toasted pecans and make gorgeous flavoursome pancakes. Do try to buy the real Canadian maple syrup, as the cheaper artificial alternatives just don't have the same rich intense flavour.

SERVES 4

### for the pancakes

2 very ripe bananas
300 ml/10 fl oz/1¼ cups buttermilk
75 g/3 oz/scant ½ cup soft brown sugar
pinch salt
25 g/1 oz/2 tbsp butter, melted
225 g/8 oz/2 cups plain (all-purpose)
   flour, sieved
75 g/3 oz/¾ cup pecan nuts, toasted

### for the butter

90 g/3½ oz/7 tbsp butter
4 tbsp maple syrup

25 g/1 oz/2 tbsp butter for frying

To make the pancakes, place the bananas in a food processor and whiz. Add the buttermilk, brown sugar, salt and melted butter and whiz again until thoroughly combined. Add the flour and whiz until you have a smooth batter. Transfer the mixture to a large bowl and stir in the pecans.

Heat a griddle or heavy-based pan and brush lightly with melted butter. Place tablespoonfuls of the mixture in the pan, leaving a little space in between each, and cook for 2–3 minutes until bubbles appear on the surface of each pancake. Carefully flip the pancakes over and cook the other sides for a further 2–3 minutes until golden brown.

Serve immediately or place the cooked pancakes on a baking tray and keep warm in the oven at 170°C/325°F/Gas 3 until required.

For the maple butter, gently heat the butter and maple syrup together until melted, stirring well.

To serve, divide the warm pancakes between 4 dessert plates and arrange in stacks. Trickle over some warm Maple Butter and serve immediately.

# soured cream and brioche pancakes
## with apricot compote

High on a hilltop near Emley Moor in North Yorkshire is a quintessential English pub called the *Three Acres* where they serve the best bread-and-butter pudding around. Crisp, buttery bread wobbles over rich vanilla custard, and a fruity apricot sauce glistens alongside. This is my version – in a pancake! For a lighter result I use brioche, a soft bread enriched with butter and eggs, but you could use good-quality ordinary white bread if you prefer.

SERVES 4

### for the pancakes

3 eggs, separated
300 ml/10 fl oz/1¼ cups soured cream
75 g/3 oz/scant ½ cup caster (superfine) sugar
40 g/1½ oz/3 tbsp butter, melted
1 tsp vanilla extract
200 ml/7 fl oz/scant 1 cup milk
200 g/7 oz brioche
2 tbsp self-raising (self-rising) flour, sieved
75 g/3 oz sultanas

### for the compote

5 tbsp water
150 g/5 oz/¾ cup caster (superfine) sugar
450 g/1 lb apricots, halved and stoned

25 g/1 oz/2 tbsp butter for frying
icing (confectioner's) sugar to dust

*continued overleaf*

To make the pancakes, place the egg yolks in a large bowl with the soured cream, caster sugar, melted butter, vanilla extract and milk, and whisk well until everything is combined and the batter is smooth. Cut the brioche into small cubes and add this to the mixture. Leave to stand for 15 minutes or so, to allow the brioche to soak up some of the batter. Using a slotted spoon, remove the soaked pieces of brioche to a separate bowl and set aside. Add the flour to the batter mixture and stir thoroughly. Return the brioche to the bowl, add the sultanas and mix well. Whisk the egg whites until stiff, then gently fold this into the mixture.

Heat a griddle or heavy-based pan and brush lightly with melted butter. Place tablespoonfuls of the mixture in the pan, leaving a little space in between each, and cook for 2–3 minutes until bubbles appear on the surface of each pancake. Carefully flip the pancakes over and cook the other sides for 2–3 minutes until golden brown.

Serve immediately or place the cooked pancakes on a baking tray and keep warm in the oven at 170°C/325°F/Gas 3 until required.

For the compote, place the water and sugar in a pan and bring to the boil, stirring to dissolve the sugar. Add the apricots to the pan and turn the heat down. Simmer for 10–15 minutes until the apricots are soft and the syrup has thickened. Leave to cool.

To serve, dust the Soured Cream and Brioche Pancakes with icing sugar and serve with Apricot Compote.

# yorkshire curd hotcakes
## with quick apricot sauce

Curd-cheese tarts are a real Yorkshire speciality and my mum makes the best! I have recreated the lovely cinnamon-sweet flavours in these fabulous hotcakes. Perfect with quick apricot sauce.

SERVES 4

### for the cakes

150 g/5 oz/generous ½ cup cottage cheese
3 eggs, separated
40 g/1½ oz/3 tbsp butter, melted
50 g/2 oz/½ cup ground almonds
40 g/1½ oz/3 tbsp caster (superfine) sugar
zest 1 orange
40 g/1½ oz/3 tbsp self-raising flour, sieved

½ tsp ground cinnamon
½ tsp ground nutmeg
50 g/2 oz/¼ cup currants

### for the sauce

175 g/6 oz good-quality apricot conserve
3 tbsp water

25 g/1 oz/2 tbsp butter for frying

Greek yoghurt to serve

To make the cakes, place the cottage cheese and egg yolks in a bowl and stir gently to mix. Add the melted butter, ground almonds, sugar and orange zest. Stir again and set aside. Mix the flour, cinnamon and nutmeg together and stir into the cheese mixture, with the currants.

Whisk the egg whites until stiff. Stir a couple of tablespoonfuls into the cake mixture then carefully fold in the remainder.

For the apricot sauce, press the conserve through a sieve into a pan with the back of a spoon. Add the water and heat gently, stirring until smooth.

Heat a griddle or heavy-based pan and brush with melted butter. Place tablespoonfuls of the mixture in the pan, leaving a little space in between each, and cook until bubbles appear on the surface of each pancake, about 2–3 minutes. Flip the cakes over and cook for 2–3 minutes, until the other sides are golden brown.

Serve immediately or place the griddle cakes on a baking tray and keep warm in the oven at 170°C/325°F/Gas 3 until required.

Serve the Yorkshire Curd Hotcakes with Quick Apricot sauce and a good dollop of Greek yoghurt.

# brandy crêpes
## with butter plum sauce

Adding a little brandy to the batter gives these crêpes a slightly crisp finish, which goes especially well with hot buttery plums.

SERVES 4

### for the crêpes

2 eggs
300 ml/10 fl oz/1¼ cups milk
40 g/1½ oz/3 tbsp caster (superfine) sugar
2 tbsp brandy
pinch salt
115 g/4 oz/1 cup plain (all-purpose) flour, sieved

### for the sauce

450 g/1 lb plums, stoned and quartered
40 g/1½ oz/3 tbsp butter
50 g/2 oz/¼ cup caster (superfine) sugar
 (or to taste)

### for the filling

115 g/4 oz/½ cup mascarpone cheese

25 g/1 oz/2 tbsp butter for frying
icing (confectioner's) to dust

To make the crêpes, place the eggs, milk, sugar, brandy and salt in a food processor and whiz until it is well mixed. Add the flour and whiz again until you have a smooth batter. Set aside for 30 minutes to an hour, longer if possible.

Lightly butter a non-stick frying pan and heat over a medium–high heat until hot. Pour in a small amount of batter (about 4 tablespoonfuls, depending on the size of your pan), tilting the pan to spread the mixture over the entire base. Cook for 1–2 minutes, until the pancake is golden on the underside and bubbles start to appear on the surface. Gently loosen the pancake around the edges and turn it over. Cook for another minute until golden brown.

Serve immediately, or if you want to keep the crêpes warm so that you can serve them all together, stack the pancakes between layers of greaseproof paper, cover them loosely in foil and place them on a baking tray in the oven at 170°C/325°F/Gas 3.

For the sauce, place the plums in a pan with the butter and sugar and cook over a gentle heat until soft. Keep warm.

To serve, spread the Brandy Crêpes with mascarpone, fold into quarters and serve with the Butter Plum Sauce.

# honey pennies

## with double oat heaven

These cute pancakes were christened 'Honey Pennies' because their size reminded me of the shiny gold-wrapped coins that are sold in the shops at Christmas time.

SERVES 4

### for the pennies

130 g/4½ oz/1 cup plus 2 tbsp self-raising (self-rising) flour, sieved
pinch salt
1 tsp baking powder
1 egg
2 tbsp honey
150 ml/5 fl oz/⅔ cup milk

### for the oats

75 g/3 oz/1 cup rolled oats
75 g/3 oz/scant 1 cup caster (superfine) sugar
1 crisp dessert apple, grated
squeeze lemon juice
350 ml/12 fl oz/1½ cups Greek yoghurt

25 g/1 oz/2 tbsp butter for frying
2 tbsp runny honey to drizzle

To make the pennies, mix the flour, salt and baking powder together in a large bowl. Whisk the egg, honey and milk together, add this to the flour and mix it all thoroughly.

For the oats, place the oats and sugar in a heavy-based pan and cook on a low heat until the sugar is dissolved and the oats are toasted. Continue to cook, stirring constantly, until the sugar caramelizes and the oats become crisp and golden. (Don't be tempted to rush this: if the heat is too high, it will burn and you will have a speckled mess!) Turn out into a bowl and leave to cool.

Mix the grated apple with the lemon juice and stir into the Greek yoghurt. Just before serving, fold in two-thirds of the crunchy oat mixture.

Heat a griddle or heavy-based pan and brush lightly with melted butter. Place teaspoonfuls of the mixture in the pan, leaving a little space in between each and cook for 1–2 minutes until bubbles appear on the surface of each penny. Carefully flip the pennies over and cook the other sides for about 1 minute more until firm, risen and golden brown.

Serve the Honey Pennies warm, topped with a dollop of the yoghurt mixture, drizzled over with a little honey and sprinkled with a little of the extra oat crunch.

# cherry and almond pancakes

When fresh cherries are in season, it's always nice to make the most of them. Their sweet, juicy flavour is perfect for crisp, custardy tarts or these charming cherry and almond pancakes. Serve them fresh and warm for breakfast or brunch, with lashings of Greek yoghurt, or relish them as a dessert with a generous dollop of ice cream.

SERVES 4

3 eggs

50 ml/2 fl oz/¹⁄₄ cup milk

25 g/1 oz butter, melted

50 g/2 oz/¹⁄₄ cup caster (superfine) sugar

115 g/4 oz/1 cup self-raising (superfine) flour, sieved

50 g/2 oz flaked almonds, lightly toasted

250 g/9 oz fresh cherries, pitted

2 tbsp butter for frying

Icing sugar to dust

Greek yoghurt or ice cream to serve

To make the pancakes, place the eggs, milk and melted butter in a large bowl and beat until smooth. Add the caster sugar and flour and stir well. Add the flaked almonds. Carefully fold in the cherries, taking care not to break them.

Heat a griddle or heavy based pan and brush lightly with melted butter.

Drop generous tablespoonfuls of the mixture into the pan, making sure to leave a little space in between each. Cook over a medium heat for about 2–3 minutes until bubbles appear on the surface of each pancake. Carefully flip the pancakes over and cook for 1–2 minutes more until the other sides are golden brown.

Serve immediately or place the cooked pancakes on a baking tray and keep warm in the oven at 170°C/325°F/Gas 3 until required.

To serve, place 4 pancakes on each of 4 dessert plates, dust with icing sugar and top with Greek yoghurt or ice cream.

# sweet sultana *poffertjes*
## with wild apricot and vanilla butter

SERVES 4

### for the *poffertjes*

130 g/4½ oz/1 cup plus 2 tbsp
self-raising (self-rising) flour,
sieved
½ tsp baking powder
pinch salt
25 g/1 oz/2 tbsp caster
  (superfine) sugar
1 egg
150 ml/5 fl oz/⅔ cup milk
½ tsp vanilla extract
1 tbsp butter, melted
50 g/2 oz sultanas

### for the butter

150 g/5 oz/1/1¼ sticks butter,
  softened slightly
250 g/9 oz/1¼ cups dried
  apricots (preferably
  unsulphured)
1 tbsp caster (superfine) sugar
1 tsp vanilla extract

25 g/1oz/2 tbsp butter
  for frying
icing (confectioner's) sugar
  to dust

This is a fruity version of the *poffertjes* (Dutch pancakes) recipe on page 26. Try to use wild apricots for this recipe if you can: they are dark and aromatic, and not treated with sulphur to preserve their colour in the way that the bright orange ones are. They make a fabulous butter with an intense flavour.

To make the *poffertjes*, mix the flour and baking powder in a large bowl and add the salt and sugar. Whisk together the egg, milk, vanilla extract and melted butter and add this to the flour mixture. Stir in the sultanas.

Heat a *poffertjes* pan, a griddle or heavy-based pan over a medium heat and brush lightly with melted butter. If you have a *poffertjes* pan, fill the little holes with batter using a teaspoon. If you are using a griddle or heavy-based pan, place teaspoonfuls of the mixture in the pan, leaving a little space in between each and cook for 1–2 minutes until bubbles appear on the surface of each *poffertje*. Carefully flip the *poffertjes* over and cook for 2–3 minutes more until firm, risen and golden brown.

Serve immediately or place the cooked pancakes on a baking tray and keep warm in the oven at 170°C/325°F/Gas 3 until required.

For the butter, place the softened butter, dried apricots, sugar and vanilla extract in a food processor and whiz to combine. When everything is well combined, turn out into a bowl and refrigerate to firm up until required.

To serve, dust the *poffertjes* with icing sugar and serve warm with Wild Apricot and Vanilla butter.

# chocolate orange crêpes
## with passion fruit sauce

Dark Chocolate Orange Crêpes and fragrant
Passion Fruit Sauce make an elegant
combination. To give the sauce an extra lift I
use concentrated orange juice (the sort that
you find in a supermarket's freezer section and
dilute to make unsweetened orange juice).
Used without diluting, it helps add a deep
orange flavour to sauces.

SERVES 4

### for the crêpes

2 eggs
300 ml/10 fl oz/1¼ cups milk
40 g/1½ oz/3 tbsp butter, melted
zest 1 orange
50 g/2 oz/¼ cup soft brown sugar
pinch salt
115 g/4 oz/1 cup plain (all-purpose) flour, sieved
1 tbsp cocoa powder, sieved

### for the sauce

6 passion fruit
3 tbsp concentrated orange juice
3 tbsp caster (superfine) sugar
2 tbsp water

25 g/1 oz/2 tbsp butter for frying
icing (confectioner's) sugar to dust

*continued overleaf*

To make the crêpes, place the eggs, milk, melted butter and orange zest in a food processor or blender. Add the brown sugar and salt and whiz until everything is well mixed. Mix the flour and cocoa powder together, add this to the egg mixture, then whiz again until you have a smooth batter. Set aside for at least 30 minutes to an hour, longer if possible.

Lightly butter a non-stick frying pan or crêpe pan and heat over a medium-high heat until hot. If the batter has thickened, it may be necessary to add a little water. Pour in a small amount of batter (about 4 tablespoonfuls depending on the size of your pan), tilting the pan to spread the mixture over the entire base. Add a little more batter if you have any holes. Cook for 1–2 minutes until the pancake is golden on the underside and bubbles start to appear on the surface. Using a palette knife, gently loosen the pancake around the edges and turn it over. Cook for another minute until golden brown. Serve immediately.

If you want to keep the crêpes warm so that you can serve them all together, stack the pancakes between layers of greaseproof paper, cover them loosely in foil and place them on a baking tray in the oven at 170°C/325°F/Gas 3.

For the sauce, cut the passion fruits in half and scoop out the seeds and pulp into a food processor. Whiz for 10 seconds or so to help release the juice from the seeds. Sieve the mixture into a small pan, reserving some of the seeds. Add the orange juice, sugar and water and heat gently until the sugar has dissolved. Stir in a few reserved seeds and set aside to cool.

To serve, fold each pancake in half, and then in half again to create a fan shape. Pour over a little Passion Fruit Sauce and dust with icing sugar. Serve immediately.

# sweet pineapple hotcake

This is a delicious combination of light and fruity pancakes with sticky, sweet Stem Ginger and Jaggery Drizzle. Jaggery, or palm sugar as it is more commonly known, is a thick, amber-coloured sugary paste used widely in South-East Asian cuisine. You can buy it in oriental stores and many large supermarkets.

SERVES 4

### for the pancakes

200 g/7 oz/scant 1 cup cottage cheese
3 eggs, separated
50 g/2 oz/¼ cup caster (superfine) sugar
pinch salt
1 tsp vanilla extract
250 g/9 oz candied pineapple, cut into large dice
25 g/1 oz/2 tbsp butter, melted
50 g/2 oz/½ cup self-raising (self-rising)
   flour, sieved

### for the drizzle

4 tbsp jaggery (palm sugar)
2 tbsp water
3 knobs preserved stem ginger, finely sliced

25 g/1 oz/2 tbsp butter for frying
icing (confectioner's) sugar to dust
Greek yoghurt to serve

To make the pancakes, place the cottage cheese and egg yolks in a large bowl and stir gently to mix. Add the caster sugar and salt. Stir in the vanilla extract, candied pineapple and melted butter. Add the flour and mix thoroughly.

Whisk the egg whites until stiff and stir a tablespoonful into the pancake mixture. Carefully fold in the remaining egg whites.

Heat a griddle or heavy-based pan and brush lightly with melted butter. Place tablespoonfuls of the mixture in the pan, leaving a little space in between each and cook for 2–3 minutes, until bubbles appear on the surface of each pancake. Carefully flip the pancakes over and cook the other sides for 2–3 minutes more until golden brown.

Serve immediately or place the cooked pancakes on a baking tray and keep warm in the oven at 170°C/325°F/Gas 3 until required.

For the drizzle, place the jaggery and water in a small pan and melt over a low heat. Add the stem ginger and stir until smooth. Keep warm.

To serve, dust the pancakes with icing sugar and serve with Greek yoghurt.

# wraps

Flour tortillas make a great-tasting and fun alternative

to traditional bread if you're after something tempting

for lunch, and preparing them at home means you can

incorporate fragrant herbs and spices. Crêpes make

wonderful wrappers, too. Fold them around warm and

chunky savoury fillings or drape them around fresh,

fruity mixtures for a sweet, mouthwatering treat.

# basic wrap recipe

Wraps (or flour tortillas) are a tasty change from bread when it comes to rustling up a special sandwich. And the good news is that they are surprisingly quick and easy to make. You can buy them ready-made in the shops, but if you make them yourself you can add any variation of aromatic herbs and spices. I have shared some of my own favourites opposite.

Don't be tempted to add any oil or butter to the pan when you cook the wraps; they should just toast lightly in a dry pan. And take care not to overcook them – although they still taste good when they are slightly crispy, they will break when you attempt to wrap them around your filling.

If necessary, keep them warm by wrapping them in foil and putting them in the oven at 150°C/300°F/Gas 2, but they are nicest served as soon as possible after cooking.

MAKES 4

150 g/5 oz/1¼ cups plain (all-purpose) flour, sieved

1 tsp salt
2 tbsp sunflower oil
4–5 tbsp water

Place the flour and salt together in a large bowl. Add the sunflower oil, then slowly add the water and stir until the mixture forms a smooth (but not sticky) dough. Knead for 3–4 minutes, then cover and leave to rest for 30 minutes or so. This stage can be done in a food processor or mixer if preferred.

When you are ready to cook the wraps, divide the dough into 4 and roll each portion out very thinly into large circles of about 25 cm/10 in diameter. Heat a large frying pan or smooth griddle until hot and cook the wraps for 20–30 seconds on each side, or until they bubble slightly and start to turn golden.

Serve immediately or keep warm in a low oven until ready to serve, as described above.

## try another flavour

*Add any of the following to the basic dough mixture:*

Soft Herb Wraps: 1 tbsp finely chopped mixed fresh herbs (such as chives, parsley, basil, etc)

Wholegrain Mustard Wraps: 2 tbsp wholegrain mustard

Cracked Pepper Wraps: 2 tsp cracked black peppercorns (use a pestle and mortar)

Garlic Wraps: 2 crushed cloves garlic

Red Pepper Wraps: half a deseeded and diced red (bell) pepper

Sesame Wraps: 1 tbsp sesame seeds

Pink Peppercorn Wraps: 1 tsp crushed, fresh pink peppercorns (use a pestle and mortar). Pink peppercorns are tiny, slightly fiery little berries preserved in brine (look for them in the spice section in larger supermarkets)

# cracked pepper wraps
## with hot pork and crackling with chilli and calvados apples

It may seem like a lot of trouble to roast a piece of pork just to make a few wraps, but if you have hungry people to feed this delicious recipe makes it worthwhile.

SERVES 4

4 warm Cracked Pepper Wraps (see page 69)

### for the apples

25 g/1 oz/2 tbsp butter
2 crisp eating apples, thinly sliced
pinch caster (superfine) sugar
pinch chilli flakes
2 tbsp Calvados brandy

### for the pork

8 good slices hot roast pork

pieces of crackling

generous handful of crisp salad leaves
 to serve

Once you have cooked the pork, the oven can be switched off, as the residual heat will keep the meat and the wraps warm while you sauté the apples. Remember to cover the wraps with foil to keep them nice and soft.

Melt the butter in a pan, then add the apples and a pinch of sugar, and sauté for 4–5 minutes until soft and golden. Stir in the chilli flakes.

Add the Calvados and set it alight. When the flames have died down, season with a little salt and freshly ground black pepper, remove from the heat and keep warm.

To serve, take a warm cracked pepper wrap and fill with some salad, 2 slices of hot pork, some crunchy crackling and a quarter of the apples. Roll up. Repeat with the other 3 and serve immediately. Standing the wraps in colourful cups enhances their impact.

# soft herb wraps
## with crispy pancetta and artichoke pesto

Crisp pancetta, smooth, creamy artichokes and salty Parmesan make a sublime trio folded inside a soft, herb-speckled wrap. You can make the artichoke pesto in advance if you wish (it's lovely with hot pasta if you have any left over). For this recipe I use cooked artichoke hearts marinated in olive oil and herbs – buy them loose from your local deli or in jars from larger supermarkets.

SERVES 4

4 warm Soft Herb Wraps (see page 69)

### for the pesto

150 g/5 oz artichokes marinated in olive oil
(drained weight)

2 fat cloves garlic

50 g/2oz/½ cup pine nuts, lightly toasted

50 g/2 oz/⅔ cup Parmesan cheese,
finely grated

zest and juice ½ lemon

salt and freshly ground black pepper

### for the filling

200 g/7 oz pancetta, finely sliced

4 generous handfuls fresh rocket leaves

To make the pesto, place all the ingredients for the pesto in the bowl of a food processor and whiz until you have a smooth paste. Season to taste. Store in the fridge until required.

Grill the pancetta for 3–4 minutes, until crisp. Keep warm.

To serve, spread a warm herb wrap generously with artichoke pesto. Scatter with some rocket leaves and place a quarter of the pancetta in the centre of the wrap. Fold 2 opposite sides of the wrap in to the centre, then fold the remaining sides in to form a parcel. Repeat with the remaining wraps and serve immediately.

# red pepper wraps
## with pastrami, soft cheese and jelly-glazed onions

Vivid speckles of ripe red pepper add a special touch to these pretty wraps. The filling is a lively combination of lightly spiced pastrami, soft cheese and sticky, savoury-sweet onions.

**MAKES 4**

4 warm Red Pepper Wraps (see page 69)

### for the onions

2 tbsp olive oil

2 large onions, halved and thinly sliced

2 tbsp balsamic vinegar

2 tbsp redcurrant jelly

salt and freshly ground black pepper

### for the filling

115 g/4 oz/½ cup soft cheese

90 g/3½ oz pastrami

First make the jelly-glazed onions. Heat the olive oil in a pan and add the onions. Cook on a low heat for 10 minutes or so until the onions are soft. Turn up the heat slightly to colour the onions a little. Add the balsamic vinegar and the redcurrant jelly, then turn the heat down and cook for a couple of minutes more until the onions are sticky and nicely glazed. Season with salt and freshly ground black pepper.

To serve, take a warm red pepper wrap and spread with soft cheese. Add a quarter of the onions and a quarter of the pastrami. Roll up. Repeat with the other 3 and present them immediately.

# wholegrain mustard wraps
## with parma ham and
## raspberry-dressed pea shoots

Wafer-thin slices of Parma ham and crisp pea shoots in raspberry dressing are a delicious combination. Pea shoots are the sweet tops from very young pea plants. They are difficult to obtain, so I grow my own. I bought a small, indoor propagator, sat it on the windowsill and threw in a handful of pea seeds. A few days later I had my own supply of tender shoots. But if you can't get hold of the shoots, use mixed salad leaves instead.

SERVES 4

4 warm Wholegrain Mustard
 Wraps (see page 69)

### for the dressing

1 tbsp raspberry vinegar
½–1 tsp caster (superfine) sugar
1 tsp wholegrain mustard
1 tbsp hazelnut oil
2 tbsp grapeseed oil
salt and freshly ground
 black pepper

### for the filling

2 generous handfuls fresh
 pea shoots
130 g/4½ oz Parma ham, very
 thinly cut

Mix the vinegar, sugar, mustard and oils together in a screw-top jar. Taste, and adjust the seasoning if necessary. Toss the pea shoots in enough dressing to coat them.

To serve, fill the warm wraps with the shoots and Parma ham and serve immediately.

# warm garlic wraps
## with smoked chicken
## and avocado

I love this combination of moist, smoky chicken and creamy avocado, snuggling inside a warm garlicky wrap. Choose succulent, good-quality chicken that has been properly smoked, rather than the bland wafer-thin slices that come in plastic cartons, labelled as sandwich cuts. If you can find a whole smoked chicken, so much the better – you can use any leftovers in a super salad the next day, or make some more garlic wraps.

SERVES 4

4 warm Garlic Wraps (see page 69)

### for the filling

2 avocados
juice ½ lime

1 clove garlic, crushed
1 tomato, deseeded and very finely diced
½ red (bell) pepper, deseeded and very
  finely diced
pinch chilli flakes
8 good plump slices smoked chicken
mixed salad leaves

To make the filling, cut the avocados in half, remove the stone, and scoop out the flesh into a large bowl. Mash it with a fork until soft but still with a little texture. Stir in the lime juice and add the garlic. Add the tomato, red pepper and chilli flakes. Mix well and season with salt and freshly ground black pepper.

To serve, take a warm garlic wrap and fill with some of the avocado mixture, some chicken and some crisp salad leaves. Roll up and serve immediately.

# cracked pepper wraps
## with roquefort, pear and honey-dressed spinach

Freshly cracked black peppercorns add an extra kick of flavour to these wraps. Use a pestle and mortar, or roll over them briefly with a rolling pin to give little crunchy pieces that have slightly more texture and bite than ground pepper. This is one of my favourite salad combinations: salty Roquefort, sweet, ripe pears and slightly peppery spinach, packaged in a tasty warm wrap.

SERVES 4

4 Cracked Pepper Wraps (see page 69)

### for the filling

75 g/3 oz young spinach leaves, washed thoroughly and dried

1 tbsp honey

1 tbsp wholegrain mustard

1 tbsp crème fraîche

1 small pear

1 tsp lemon juice

130 g/4½ oz Roquefort cheese, crumbled

To make the filling, pile the spinach leaves into a large bowl. Place the honey, mustard and crème fraîche in a separate bowl and stir until thoroughly mixed. Set aside. Cut the pear in half (no need to peel it). Using a potato peeler, shave fine slices of pear, toss them in a little lemon juice (to prevent discoloration) and add these to the spinach. Add the Roquefort. Toss the salad in enough dressing to coat the leaves lightly.

To serve, pile into warm cracked pepper wraps. Roll up and serve immediately.

# sesame wraps
## with honey and tamarind chicken and oriental salad

The long, brown pods of the tamarind tree yield a bitter sweet flesh, flecked with dark seeds, which is often sold in hard, compressed blocks to be diluted with water to give tamarind juice. It is used extensively in Indian and Chinese cuisine, and imparts a tangy, almost sour flavour. For convenience I buy the ready-prepared paste that is now quite easy to find in the spice section of supermarkets and delicatessens. The sharp flavour of tamarind combines well with sticky, sweet honey and makes a lush glaze for chicken.

To prepare the chicken, cut the chicken into thin strips and lay the pieces in a shallow dish. Mix the garlic, honey, soy sauce, tamarind paste, mustard, lime and seasoning together. Pour this mixture over the chicken and leave to marinate for 30 minutes or so. Lift the chicken out of the marinade and grill for 8–10 minutes until cooked through and golden, basting with the leftover marinade from time to time. Remove from the heat and keep warm.

For the the dressing, mix the stem ginger, ginger syrup, soy sauce and groundnut oil together in a screw-top jar and shake until thoroughly mixed. Toss the salad ingredients together and coat lightly with dressing.

To serve, divide the salad and chicken between 4 warm wraps, roll up and serve immediately.

SERVES 4

4 warm Sesame Wraps (see page 69)

### for the chicken

4 small boneless chicken breasts, skinned
1 clove garlic, crushed
1 tbsp honey
1 tbsp soy sauce
1 tbsp tamarind paste
1 tbsp mustard
squeeze lime juice
salt and freshly ground black pepper

### for the dressing

1 knob preserved stem ginger, finely chopped
1 tbsp preserved stem ginger syrup
1 tbsp soy sauce
1 tbsp groundnut oil

### for the salad

4 spring onions (scallions) cut into strips, lengthways
generous handful beansprouts
generous handful sugar-snaps, cut in half lengthways
1 small carrot, shaved into ribbons with a potato peeler
½ red (bell) pepper, cut into strips
2 good handfuls Chinese leaf

# pink peppercorn wraps
## with roasted red pepper, feta and olive salad

An amazing transformation takes place when red peppers are oven-roasted with garlic and olive oil. They become meltingly soft and tender and packed with flavour – beautiful with crumbly feta cheese, salty black olives and pungent basil pesto.

SERVES 4

4 warm Pink Peppercorn Wraps (see page 69)

12 black olives, pitted

2 tbsp good-quality balsamic vinegar

### for the salad

6 red (bell) peppers, topped and tailed

5 tbsp olive oil (I often use a chilli-infused oil)

2 cloves garlic, crushed

salt and freshly ground black pepper

250 g/9 oz feta cheese, crumbled

### for the pesto

2 generous handfuls basil leaves

50 g/2 oz/²⁄₃ cup Parmesan, grated

50 g/2 oz/¹⁄₂ cup pine nuts

2 cloves garlic, crushed

1 tbsp fresh lemon juice

4 tbsp olive oil

Preheat the oven to 200°/400°F/Gas 6.

To make the salad, cut the peppers into thin strips. Place in a shallow ovenproof dish or roasting tin. Dribble over the olive oil, scatter with garlic and toss the peppers around a little until everything is nicely coated. Season with salt and freshly ground black pepper. Roast for 30–40 minutes until soft and charred slightly here and there. Turn into a shallow dish and leave to cool. When the peppers have reached room temperature, sprinkle with the feta cheese. Scatter with the olives, check the seasoning and drizzle over balsamic vinegar.

For the pesto, place the basil, Parmesan, pine nuts, garlic and lemon in the bowl of a food processor. Whiz to combine. Add enough olive oil to give a lightly textured paste. Store in a screw-top jar and refrigerate until ready to use.

To serve, spread a little pesto on to each of 4 warm pink peppercorn wraps, fill with Roasted Red Pepper, Feta and Olive Salad and serve immediately.

# soft herb wraps
## with prawns and asparagus with lemon mayonnaise

These are great wraps to enjoy with newly picked home-grown asparagus. Eggs also have a natural affinity with asparagus, so you could substitute hard-boiled eggs in place of the prawns if you prefer. Homemade mayonnaise is very quick to make, and the good news is that you can make it in advance then store it in the fridge until you're ready to wrap!

SERVES 4

4 Soft Herb Wraps (see page 69)

### for the mayonnaise

1 egg
zest 2 lemons
juice 1 lemon
1 tsp Dijon mustard
300 ml/10 fl oz/1¼ cups light olive oil
salt and freshly ground black pepper

### for the filling

200 g/7 oz cooked prawns
150 g/5 oz young asparagus, lightly cooked
assorted salad leaves

To make the mayonnaise, place the egg, lemon zest, 1 tbsp lemon juice, mustard and salt in the bowl of a blender. Whiz to combine. With the motor running, begin to trickle in the olive oil slowly until you have added about a third, then add the remaining oil more quickly. When all the oil has been incorporated, add the remaining lemon juice and adjust the seasoning, adding a little more salt if necessary, and a little freshly ground black pepper. Whiz again to blend.

For the filling mix 3–4 tbsp mayonnaise with the prawn.

To serve, fill the wraps with some of the prawn mixture, a few spears of cooked asparagus and a handful of fresh salad leaves. Roll up and serve immediately.

# strawberry and kiwi wraps
## with mango and malibu sauce

Vibrant colours and fruity, summer flavours make this a dazzling dessert. Juicy chunks of sweet pineapple make a good substitute for the strawberries as a change. The sauce can be made in advance.

SERVES 4

4 Basic Sweet Crêpes (see page 42)

### for the sauce

300 g/11 oz fresh mango pulp

4 tbsp Malibu liqueur

75 g/3 oz/scant 1 cup caster (superfine) sugar

### for the filling

3 kiwi fruit, peeled and thinly sliced

250 g/9 oz/2 cups strawberries, washed and thinly sliced

### for the topping

50 g/2 oz/½ cup pistachios, shelled and roughly chopped

icing (confectioner's) sugar to dust

To make the sauce, put the mango pulp in the bowl of a food processor with the Malibu liqueur and caster sugar. Whiz until you have a smooth sauce. Set aside.

To serve, lay a crêpe out flat and place a few strawberry and kiwi slices in the centre. Loosely fold the edges of the crêpe a little way into the centre, leaving most of the fruit exposed. Repeat with the other crêpes, then place on 4 serving plates, scatter with the chopped pistachios, sprinkle with icing sugar and surround with Mango and Malibu Sauce.

# sweet lemon *crespelle*

A *crespelle* is an Italian crêpe, wrapped around a tasty filling and baked in the oven until puffed up and golden. This sweet variation is saucy, lemony and light. Fresh blackberries make a luscious accompaniment, but you can substitute your own favourite berries or vary them according to the season.

SERVES 4

### for the *crespelle*

2 eggs
300 ml/10 fl oz/1¼ cups milk
40 g/1½ oz/3 tbsp butter, melted
40 g/1½ oz/3 tbsp caster (superfine) sugar
zest 2 lemons
pinch salt
115 g/4 oz/1 cup plain (all-purpose) flour, sieved

### for the filling

350 g/12 oz/1½ cups ricotta cheese
zest and juice 1½ lemons
90 g/3½ oz/7 tbsp caster (superfine) sugar
40 g/1½ oz/scant ½ cups ground almonds

### for the sauce

75 g/3 oz/6 tbsp butter
juice 1½ lemons
150 g/5 oz/1¼ cups icing (confectioner's) sugar
4 tbsp water
25 g/1 oz/2 tbsp butter for frying
15 g/½ oz/1 tbsp butter, melted, for greasing the dish
blackberries to garnish
icing (confectioner's) sugar to dust

 continued overleaf

Preheat the oven to 180°C/350°F/Gas 4.

To make the crêpes, place the eggs, milk and melted butter in a food processor or blender. Add the sugar, lemon zest and a pinch of salt and whiz until everything is well mixed. Add the flour and whiz again until you have a smooth batter. Set aside for 30 minutes to an hour, longer if possible.

Lightly butter a non-stick frying pan or crêpe pan and heat over a medium high heat until hot. If the batter has thickened, it may be necessary to add a little water. Pour in a small amount of batter (about 4 tbsp depending on the size of you pan), tilting the pan to spread the mixture over the entire base. Add a little more batter if you have any holes. Cook for 1–2 minutes, until the pancake is golden on the underside, and bubbles start to appear on the surface. Using a palette knife, gently loosen the crêpe around the edges and turn it over. Cook for a further minute until golden brown.

Stack the crêpes between layers of greaseproof paper and set aside.

Now make the filling for the *crespelle*. Beat the ricotta cheese, lemon zest and juice and sugar together in a large bowl. Add the ground almonds.

Lightly brush an ovenproof dish with melted butter. Lay a cooked crêpe out flat and put a generous spoonful of the cheese mixture into the centre of the crêpe. Fold in the 2 opposite sides and then fold in the top and bottom. Turn the *crespelle* over and place seam-side down in the prepared dish. Repeat with the remaining crêpes.

For the sauce, place the butter, lemon juice, icing sugar and water in a small pan and heat gently until melted. Pour this over the *crespelle*. Place in the oven for 15 minutes until golden brown and coated in a sticky lemon glaze.

Serve immediately, garnished with fresh blackberries and dusted with icing sugar.

# glazed rum and chestnut wraps

Dark Jamaican rum and sweet chestnut purée make a scrumptious filling for wraps that takes next to no time to prepare. Scattering the wraps with sugar and grilling them until the sugar melts to a crunchy caramel glaze creates the perfect finish.

SERVES 4

8 Basic Sweet Crêpes (see page 42)

450g/ 1 lb sweetened chestnut purée

3 tbsp dark Jamaican rum

15g/½oz/1 tbsp butter, melted

4 tbsp icing sugar, sieved

freshly whipped cream or ice cream to serve

To make the filling, mix together the chestnut purée and rum until thoroughly combined. Spread a thin layer of the chestnut filling on to a crêpe, then fold it in half and then in half again to create a fan shape. Brush a large, shallow ovenproof dish with melted butter and place the crêpe in it. Repeat with the remaining 7 crêpes.

Sprinkle the icing sugar evenly over the crêpes, then place under a hot grill for 1–2 minutes until the sugar has melted and caramelized.

Serve immediately with freshly whipped cream or a dollop of vanilla ice cream (see page 90).

# normandy wraps
## with calvados apples and crème fraîche

Normandy is such a picturesque part of France, and is renowned for the production of Calvados, a brandy distilled from cider, as well as exquisite creamy milk that is used to make wonderful butter and cream. All these flavours are combined here, to create a truly scrumptious crêpe.

SERVES 4

8 Basic Sweet Crêpes (see page 42)

### for the filling

40 g/1½ oz/3 tbsp butter
8 crisp, well-flavoured eating apples, cored and sliced
75 g/3 oz/scant 1 cup caster (superfine) sugar
2 tbsp Calvados brandy

flaked almonds, to sprinkle
icing (confectioner's) sugar to dust
crème fraîche to serve

To make the filling, melt the butter in a heavy-based pan and sauté the apple slices until golden. Add the sugar and cook gently until soft. Pour in the Calvados and set it alight. Remove from the heat and allow the flames to subside.

To serve, divide the apples between the crêpes and fold into fan shapes. Sprinkle with some flaked almonds, dust with icing sugar and serve immediately with chilled crème fraiche.

# coffee grain wraps
## with ice cream and irish cream

Adding freckles of crushed, fresh coffee beans to crêpe batter gives the finished crêpe a lovely crunchy texture. Rich vanilla ice cream and a generous drizzle of Irish cream liqueur turn quite a simple combination into a really lush dessert. Make the ice cream in advance to allow for freezing.

SERVES 4

### for the crêpes

40 g/1½ oz fresh coffee beans
3 eggs
40 g/1½ oz/3 tbsp butter, melted
300 ml/10 fl oz/1¼ cups milk
1 tbsp rum
50 g/2 oz/¼ cup soft brown sugar
pinch salt
115 g/4 oz/1 cup plain (all-purpose) flour, sieved

### for the ice cream

6 egg yolks
175 g/6 oz/⅞ cup caster (superfine) sugar
2 plump vanilla pods
450 ml/15 fl oz/scant 2 cups milk
300 ml/10 fl oz/1¼ cups double (heavy) cream

25 g/1 oz/2 tbsp butter for frying
8 tbsp Irish whiskey cream liqueur to drizzle
icing (confectioner's) sugar to dust

    *continued overleaf*

To make the crêpes, place the coffee beans in a food processor and whiz until they are broken up into tiny pieces. Add the eggs, melted butter, milk and rum and whiz until everything is well combined. Add the sugar, salt and flour to the mixture and whiz until you have a smooth batter. Leave to stand for 30 minutes to an hour, longer if possible.

Lightly butter a non-stick frying pan or crêpe pan and heat over a medium-high heat until hot. If the batter has thickened, it may be necessary to add a little water. Pour in a small amount of batter (about 4 tbsp depending on the size of your pan), tilting the pan to spread the mixture over the entire base. Add a little more batter if you have any holes. Cook for 1–2 minutes, until the pancake is golden on the underside and bubbles start to appear on the surface. Using a palette knife, gently loosen the crêpe around the edges and turn it over. Cook for another minute until golden brown.

If you want to keep the crêpes warm so that you can serve them all together, stack them between layers of greaseproof paper, cover them loosely in foil and place them on a baking tray in the oven at 170°C/325°F/Gas 3.

For the ice cream, place the egg yolks in a bowl and add the sugar. Cut the vanilla pods open down the centre but leave the top ends intact. Scrape out the seeds and add to the egg-and-sugar mixture. Stir well until the mixture is smooth and light.

Put the vanilla pods and milk into a saucepan and heat until just below boiling. Pour the hot milk into the egg mixture and stir. Carefully pour everything back into the pan and stir constantly over a gentle heat with a wooden spoon until the custard is thick enough to coat the back of the spoon. Remove from the heat. Add the double cream. Leave to cool, then freeze in an ice cream machine.

To serve, place a warm crêpe on a dessert plate and spoon a liberal dollop of ice cream in the centre. Fold the edges of the crêpe in to the centre, leaving some of the ice cream exposed. Drizzle with the Irish whiskey liqueur, dust with icing sugar and serve immediately.

# chocolate and pear wraps
## with spiced sugar and mascarpone

This fabulous but simple recipe came about at the end of a frantic breakfast time when I had a lot of hungry mouths to feed! Chocolate crêpes were on the menu and were disappearing fast! When the satisfied diners had left the table, there was one chocolate crêpe left and so I sat myself down with a fresh coffee, spread Mascarpone liberally over the crêpe and wrapped it around some freshly sliced pear. Now it's become a favourite thing to do – and is brilliant with all manner of different fruit.

MAKES 8

8 chocolate crêpes (follow the recipe for
   chocolate orange crêpes on page 63 but
   omit the orange zest)
2 tbsp caster (superfine) sugar
1 tsp ground cinnamon

250 g/9 oz Mascarpone
4 medium ripe but firm pears, washed,
   cored and thinly sliced

icing sugar to dust (optional)

Mix together the caster sugar and cinnamon in a small bowl and set aside. Take a chocolate crêpes and spread it liberally with the Mascarpone. Sprinkle over a little of the spiced sugar. Place some pears slices along the centre of the crêpe. Fold the bottom edge upwards and the two sides in towards the centre, wrapping the pears neatly in much the same way as when making a tortilla wrap. Repeat with the remaining crêpes, dust with a little icing sugar if desired and serve immediately.

# rolls

When it comes to fabulous crêpes and pancakes, there
are some you stack, some you wrap and the rest – you
roll! A light crêpe makes a wonderfully chic alternative
to pasta in traditional Italian dishes such as *cannelloni*.
A beautiful filling glinting intriguingly inside a lacy
crêpe can create a delicious meal that is as informal or
as fancy as the occasion requires.

# spicy prawn and fontina rolls

This makes such a tasty supper and is surprisingly simple and quick to make. In fact, if you have some crêpes in the freezer, they can be rustled up in a matter of minutes. Fontina is an Italian cheese with a sweet, nutty flavour and a texture that makes it especially good for melting. Take care to choose good-quality, plump prawns; if you are using frozen prawns, be wary of the cheaper frozen brands that wither away to nothing when defrosted.

SERVES 4

8 Poppy Seed Crêpes (see page 15)

### for the filling

200 ml/7 fl oz/scant 1 cup double
  (heavy) cream
400 g/14 oz cooked, peeled prawns
1 tbsp Worcester sauce
shake of Tabasco sauce (optional)

2 tomatoes, deseeded and very finely diced
2 tbsp fresh coriander (cilantro),
finely chopped

### for the topping

200 g/7 oz Fontina cheese, grated

15 g/½ oz/1 tbsp butter for greasing an
  ovenproof dish

To make the filling, whisk the double cream very lightly until it thickens slightly. Add the prawns, Worcester sauce and Tabasco (if using). Add the chopped tomatoes and coriander and stir well.

Lightly brush an ovenproof dish with melted butter. Spoon a little of the prawn mixture on the centre of a Poppy Seed Crêpe and roll up. Place the rolled crêpe in the prepared dish. Repeat with the other 7 crêpes, making sure that they sit snugly together. Scatter over the grated Fontina cheese and grill for 2–3 minutes or until the cheese is golden brown and bubbling.

Serve immediately.

# broccoli, bacon and blue cheese rolls

Freshly cooked broccoli, piquant blue cheese and crisp, salty bacon make this a really tasty supper dish.

SERVES 4

8 Cracked Pepper Crêpes (see page 15)

### for the filling

750 g/1 lb 10 oz broccoli, lightly cooked and drained

2 tbsp olive oil

1 red onion, finely chopped

6 mushrooms, finely sliced

90 g/3½ oz cubed pancetta or bacon lardons

300 ml/10 fl oz/1¼ cups milk

25 g/1 oz/2 tbsp butter

25 g/1 oz/¼ cup plain (all-purpose) flour

2 tsp wholegrain mustard

130 g/4½ oz Roquefort cheese, crumbled

25 g/1 oz/¼ cup pine nuts

### for the topping

50 g/2 oz/⅔ cup Parmesan cheese, grated

15 g/½ oz/1 tbsp butter, melted, for greasing an ovenproof dish

salad leaves to serve

Preheat the oven to 190°C/375°F/Gas 5.

To make the filling, place the broccoli in a bowl. Heat the olive oil in a pan and sauté the onion and mushrooms until soft. Add the pancetta and cook for 4–5 minutes. Remove from heat and drain on kitchen paper, then add to the broccoli.

Heat the milk until just below boiling point. Melt the butter in a separate pan and add the flour. Stir over a low heat for 2–3 minutes taking care that the mixture doesn't turn brown. Slowly add the hot milk, and continue stirring until the sauce is smooth. Simmer and keep stirring until the sauce thickens. Add the mustard then pour the sauce into the bowl with the broccoli, onions, mushrooms and bacon. Add 75 g/3 oz Roquefort to the mixture and stir this into the sauce.

Allow the sauce to cool slightly, then crumble the remaining cheese into the bowl. This will create nuggets of molten cheese. Gently fold in the pine nuts.

Lightly brush an ovenproof dish with melted butter. Fill the crêpes with the broccoli mixture, roll them up and place them in the dish. Sprinkle with Parmesan cheese, cover lightly with foil and bake in the oven until hot.

Serve immediately with a green salad.

# black olive rolls
## with roasted vegetables

These rolls have a delicious flavour that goes especially well with oven-roasted vegetables. Cut the vegetables into chunky dice of a similar size so that they cook evenly.

SERVES 4

8 Black Olive Crêpes (see page 15)

### for the vegetables

1 large red onion, cut into chunky dice

1 orange (bell) pepper, topped, tailed and cut into chunky dice

1 yellow (bell) pepper, topped, tailed and cut into chunky dice

1 red (bell) pepper, topped, tailed and cut into chunky dice

1 medium aubergine (eggplant), topped, tailed and cut into chunky dice

2 medium courgettes (zucchini), sliced

4 ripe tomatoes, cut into chunky dice

2 cloves garlic, crushed

2–3 sprigs fresh thyme

4 tbsp olive oil

salt and freshly ground black pepper

8 sun-dried tomatoes, roughly chopped

2 tbsp balsamic vinegar

handful fresh basil leaves, torn

### for the topping

50 g/2 oz/²⁄₃ cup Parmesan cheese, finely grated

15 g/¹⁄₂ oz/1 tbsp butter for greasing an ovenproof dish

fresh basil to garnish

green salad to serve

Preheat the oven 190°C/375°F/Gas 5.

To make the filling, place all the vegetables except the sun-dried tomatoes on a large baking tray. Sprinkle with the garlic and lay the sprigs of thyme on top. Drizzle over the olive oil. Season with salt and pepper. Cook for about 50 minutes, or until the vegetables are turning dark golden brown. Remove from the oven and add the sun-dried tomatoes. Return to the oven for a further 10 minutes, then remove and drizzle over the vinegar. Add the basil leaves and stir into the vegetables.

Brush an ovenproof dish with melted butter. Wrap up some of the vegetable mixture in an Olive Crêpe and place it in the dish. Repeat with the other 7 crêpes. Scatter with the grated Parmesan and bake for 10–15 minutes.

To serve, place 2 Black Olive Rolls on each plate, garnish with fresh basil and serve immediately with a crisp green salad.

# spinach and ricotta rolls
## with rich tomato sauce

Ricotta cheese is a soft, white Italian cheese with a mild flavour that is used widely in both savoury and sweet dishes. Spinach and ricotta *cannelloni* is a classic Italian pasta dish, in which rolls of pasta are filled with a mixture of spinach, tomatoes and ricotta. I think these rolls work perfectly in place of pasta.

Preheat the oven to 180°C/350°F/Gas 4.

To make the filling, heat the olive oil in a pan and gently sauté the shallots until soft but not coloured. Add the crushed garlic. Cook for a minute more and then remove from the heat. Wash the spinach and place in a large pan with just the water droplets still clinging. Add the butter and sauté for 2–3 minutes until the spinach wilts and is soft. Remove from the heat, drain the spinach in a colander and squeeze it to remove any remaining water. Chop the spinach and put it in a bowl with the shallots and garlic. Add the tomatoes. Stir in the ricotta cheese and add the nutmeg. Season with salt and freshly ground black pepper.

For the tomato sauce, heat the oil in a pan and sauté the onion and garlic until soft but not brown. Stir in the tinned tomatoes and sugar. Tear the fresh basil leaves into small pieces and add half to the pan. Let everything bubble down for about 20 minutes or so until the sauce is thick. Season with salt and freshly ground black pepper. Remove from the heat and add the remaining basil.

Lightly brush an ovenproof dish with melted butter. Fill the crêpes with the ricotta mixture and roll them up. Lay them in the dish and pour over the tomato sauce. Sprinkle with Parmesan and bake for 15–20 minutes until hot and bubbling.

SERVES 4

8 Basic Crêpes (see page 14)

## for the filling

2 tbsp olive oil

3 shallots, peeled and finely chopped

1 clove garlic, crushed

350 g/12 oz young spinach leaves

15 g/½ oz/1 tbsp butter

6 tomatoes, deseeded and finely chopped

300 g/11 oz/scant 1½ cups ricotta cheese

pinch freshly grated nutmeg

## for the sauce

2 tbsp olive oil

1 large onion, finely chopped

2 cloves garlic, crushed

2 × 400 g/14 oz/large tins chopped tomatoes

1 tsp caster (superfine) sugar

handful fresh basil leaves

salt and freshly ground black pepper

## for the topping

50 g/2 oz/⅔ cup Parmesan cheese, finely grated

15 g/½ oz/1 tbsp butter for greasing an ovenproof dish

# Chinese spring rolls
## with quick crispy duck

Making the thin, pale golden pancakes served in Chinese restaurants is easy to do at home, and these are especially nice studded with tiny sesame seeds. The traditional method of producing crispy duck involves hanging it up for hours to dry, but this cheat's version is much quicker and produces an extremely tasty and crisp alternative.

SERVES 4

### for the pancakes

115 g/4 oz/1 cup plain (all-purpose) flour
1 tbsp sesame seeds
7–8 tbsp boiling water
2 tsp toasted sesame oil

### for the duck

4–6 duck legs
900 ml/1½ pt/3¾ cups chicken stock
2 tsp Chinese five-spice powder
2 pieces star anise
1 bay leaf
1 tbsp honey
1 tbsp sherry
1 tbsp Indonesian sweet soy sauce
 (ketjap manis)
pinch salt

### for the plum sauce

2 tablespoons good-quality plum conserve
1 tablespoon Indonesian sweet soy sauce
 (ketjap manis)
1 tsp sherry

½ cucumber, seeds removed and cut into
 batons of about 10 cm/4 in
8 spring onions (scallions), sliced lengthways

To make the pancakes, place the flour and sesame seeds in a large bowl. Carefully add the boiling water and mix until the mixture forms a dough. Knead for 4–5 minutes until smooth (this can be done in a food mixer or processor). Cover the dough and leave it to rest for 20 minutes or so.

To cook the pancakes, take pieces of dough roughly the size of large walnuts and roll out into thin circles of about 13 cm/5 in diameter. Keep the rolled pancakes covered with a damp teatowel to prevent them from drying out.

Cook the pancakes in pairs (this stops them from drying out). To do this, brush the top of 1 pancake with a little sesame oil and top with a second pancake. Roll the 2 out together until the diameter is increased to 15 cm/6 in diameter. Lightly oil a heavy-based frying pan and cook the pancakes for 20–30 seconds on each side until they are light golden brown and blistered here and there. Remove from the pan and gently ease the 2 pancakes apart. Serve straight away, or stack them on a plate, cover them with foil and place the plate over a pan of simmering water to keep them warm until you are ready to serve.

In the meantime, prepare the crispy duck. Place the duck legs in a large pan and cover with the stock. Add the five-spice powder, star anise and bay leaf. Bring to the boil, then turn down the heat and simmer for 1 hour. Remove the duck legs from the stock, take all the meat off the bones and shred it by pulling it apart with 2 forks. Set aside. In a large bowl, mix the honey, sherry and sweet soy sauce together with a pinch of salt. Add the duck meat and stir until the duck is thoroughly coated. Spread the duck meat out in a large grill pan, then cook under a hot grill until brown and crisp.

For the plum sauce, press the plum conserve through a fine sieve with the back of a spoon. Add the soy sauce and sherry and stir until smooth. Set aside.

To serve, spread a little of the plum sauce onto each pancake, fill with some batons of cucumber, some spring onions and a little crispy duck. Roll up and serve immediately.

# tutti frutti blintzes
## with blackcurrant sauce

Blintzes are essentially little packages made from crêpes that have been cooked on one side only, then filled and fried in butter until crisp. I find it much easier, but equally delicious, to drizzle them with butter and bake them in the oven. Try to use good-quality candied fruit to fill these tempting parcels. If you have difficulty getting hold of it, the packets of ready-to-eat mixed dried exotic fruit that are easily available now would be a good substitute.

SERVES 4

8 Sweet Crêpes (see page 42)

### for the filling

350 g/12 oz/1½ cups cream cheese

50 g/2 oz/¼ cup caster (superfine) sugar

2 egg yolks

1 tbsp Grand Marnier liqueur

zest 1 orange

115 g/4 oz/⅔ cup mixed candied fruit, diced

### for the glaze

50 g/2 oz/¼ cup butter, melted

### for the sauce

175 g/6 oz good-quality blackcurrant conserve

3 tbsp water

15 g/½ oz/1 tbsp butter for greasing an ovenproof dish

icing (confectioner's) sugar to dust

Preheat the oven to 180°C/350°F/Gas 4.

To make the filling for the blintzes, beat the cream cheese, caster sugar, egg yolks, Grand Marnier liqueur and orange juice together in a large bowl. Add the diced candied fruits.

Lightly brush an ovenproof dish with melted butter. Lay a crêpe out flat and put a generous spoonful of the cheese mixture in the centre. Fold in the 2 opposite sides and then fold in the top and bottom. Turn the blintz over and place seam-side down in the prepared dish. Repeat with the remaining crêpes. Brush generously with melted butter and cover with foil. Bake for 15–20 minutes until heated through.

For the sauce, place the blackcurrant conserve with the water in a small pan, and heat gently, stirring constantly. Remove from the heat and keep warm.

To serve, place 2 Tutti Frutti Blintzes on each plate, drizzle with Blackcurrant Sauce, dust with icing sugar and serve immediately.

# banoffi rolls

## with butterscotch sauce

I love the idea of Banoffi Pie but always find the usual version far too sweet, so here I've combined all the best elements of the dessert in a deliciously different way. Ripe bananas folded into lashings of whipped cream, wrapped inside a crêpe and dribbled with a sticky butterscotch sauce make a truly decadent end to a meal. You can make the butterscotch sauce in advance if you prefer.

SERVES 4

8 Sweet Crêpes (see page 42)

### for the sauce

115 g/4 oz/½ cup caster (superfine) sugar

1 tbsp golden syrup

150 ml/5 fl oz/⅔ cup double (heavy) cream

### for the filling

4 ripe bananas

squeeze lemon juice

300 ml/10 fl oz/1¼ cups whipping cream

75 g/3 oz honey-glazed banana chips, roughly chopped, to sprinkle

icing (confectioner's) sugar to dust

To make the butterscotch sauce, place the caster sugar and golden syrup into a small heavy-based pan over a gentle heat and stir until the sugar is dissolved. Let the mixture bubble until it begins to turn a dark caramel colour (but not too dark – burnt caramel tastes bitter). Remove the pan from the heat and, holding it away from you, carefully add the cream. The mixture will splatter and hot caramel will burn, so be very careful. Stir the mixture with a wooden spoon until the cream has melted into the hot caramel and the sauce is smooth. Leave to cool.

For the filling, peel and slice the bananas and place them in a bowl with a little squeeze of lemon juice to prevent discoloration. Whip the cream until it forms soft peaks, then carefully fold in the bananas. Fill the crêpes with this mixture and roll them up.

To serve, drizzle some Butterscotch Sauce over and around the crêpes. Scatter with a few chopped banana chips, dust with icing sugar and serve immediately.

# lime and lemon roll-ups

The filling for these zesty crêpes is so tangy and mouthwatering they always disappear in seconds, to rave reviews. The beauty of them is that they are so very simple to do. You'll be surprised how quickly the cream thickens to a mousse-like texture when the lemon and lime juices are added, and caramelizing the tops gives them a really nice finish.

SERVES 4

8 Sweet Crêpes (see page 42)

### for the filling

150 ml/5 fl oz/²⁄₃ cup double (heavy) cream

1 × 175 g/6 oz/small tin condensed milk

zest and juice 1½ lemons

juice ½ lime

50 g/2 oz/½ cup flaked almonds to sprinkle

icing (confectioner's) sugar to dust

To make the filling, whisk the double cream, condensed milk, lemon zest and juice and lime juice together until the mixture is thick. Fill the crêpes with this mixture and roll them up.

To serve, place 2 rolls, side by side, on each of 4 heatproof dessert plates, scatter with some flaked almonds, dust with icing sugar, grill to caramelize the tops and serve immediately.

rolls

# coconut lace rolls
## with tropical fruit salsa and sweet rum mascarpone

Crêpes *dentelles* are delightful lace pancakes served as a speciality in parts of France. Here I have used a similar idea, adding coconut to the batter and filling them with a lovely salsa that is brimming with exotic flavours. Creamy mascarpone, slightly sweetened and laced with dark rum makes the perfect accompaniment.

SERVES 4

### for the crêpes

3 eggs, lightly beaten
pinch salt
350 ml/12 fl oz/1¼ cups milk
90 g/3½ oz/⅔ cup plain (all-purpose) flour
50g/2 oz/¼ cup caster (superfine) sugar
50 g/2 oz desiccated coconut
50 g/2 oz/¼ cup butter, melted

### for the salsa

1 medium mango, peeled and cut into
   medium dice
1 papaya (paw paw), peeled, seeded and cut
   into medium dice
4 ripe kiwi fruit, peeled and thinly sliced
1 small pineapple, peeled and cut into
   medium dice
1 banana, peeled and thinly sliced
2 passion fruits
zest and juice ½ lime
50 g/2 oz/¼ cup caster (superfine) sugar
   (or to taste)

### for the rum mascarpone

250 g/9 oz/scant 1¼ cups mascarpone
4–5 tbsp caster (superfine) sugar (or to taste)
3 tbsp dark rum (or to taste)

50 g/2 oz/¼ cup butter for frying
icing (confectioner's) sugar and cocoa powder
   for dusting

*continued overleaf*

Prepare the crêpe batter first. Place the eggs, salt and milk in a food processor and whiz. Sieve the flour, then add the sugar and coconut. Add this to the egg mixture and whiz again until you have a smooth batter. Trickle in the melted butter and leave the mixture to stand for at least an hour.

Make the salsa 30 minutes or so in advance to allow the flavours to develop. Toss the evenly diced and sliced fruit together in a large bowl. Squeeze the juice and seeds out of the passion fruits and add to the bowl (you can remove the seeds if you're not keen on the crunchy texture!). Add the lime zest and juice, with the sugar. You may need to adjust the quantity of sugar according to the ripeness of your fruit. Stir well and set aside to marinate for 10–15 minutes.

When you are ready to cook the crêpes, lightly butter a non-stick frying pan or crêpe pan and heat over a medium–high heat until hot. Using a ladle, trickle about 3 tbsp batter (depending on the size of your pan) into the pan, rotating the pan at the same time in order to create a lacy effect. When the batter has set, after about 1 minute, gently lift it with a palette knife and carefully turn it over. Cook the reverse side for 30 seconds or so until golden. Repeat with the remaining batter.

If you want to keep the crêpes warm so that you can serve them all together, stack the pancakes between layers of greaseproof paper, cover them loosely with foil and place them on a baking tray in the oven at 170°C/325°F/Gas 3.

For the rum mascarpone, put the mascarpone, sugar and rum into a small pan and heat very gently to warm through. Taste, and adjust the rum and sugar if necessary.

To serve, spoon some of the salsa on the centre of each crêpe and carefully roll up. Divide the rum mascarpone between 4 plates. Lay a crêpe carefully in the centre of each plate. Dust with icing sugar and a little cocoa powder and serve immediately.

# peaches 'n' praline
## cream rolls

Fresh peaches with cream are a favourite summer treat. Adding a touch of crunchy praline and rolling them up inside golden crêpes adds a special touch. Make the praline in advance and keep it in an airtight jar until you are ready to serve. I often make extra and keep it in the fridge – it's lovely sprinkled over ice cream.

SERVES 4

8 Sweet Crêpes (see page 42)

### for the praline

50 g/2 oz/¼ cup caster (superfine) sugar
50 g/2 oz/½ cup flaked almonds

### for the filling

2 ripe but firm peaches
300 ml/10 fl oz/1¼ cups double (heavy) cream
50 g/2 oz/½ cup icing (confectioner's) sugar
2 tbsp peach liqueur

50 g/2oz/½ cup flaked almonds to sprinkle
icing (confectioner's) sugar to dust

You will need a lightly buttered baking tray

To make the praline, heat the sugar in a heavy-based pan until it dissolves and turns a golden caramel colour. Remove from the heat and add the flaked almonds. Return to the heat for a few seconds to lightly toast the almonds, stirring all the time. Turn out the mixture carefully into the baking tray, spread it out evenly, then leave to cool. When it is completely cold, break the mixture up and crush into a slightly textured powder using a rolling pin (simply whizzing in a food processor will do the same job).

For the filling, wash the peaches, remove the stones and cut into fairly large dice. Whisk the cream, sugar and peach liqueur together until the mixture forms soft peaks, then stir in the peach dice and fold in the almond praline. Fill the crêpes with this mixture and roll up.

To serve, place 2 rolls, side by side, on each of 4 heatproof dessert plates, sprinkle with some flaked almonds and a little icing sugar, grill briefly to caramelize (take care not to scorch the tops!) and serve immediately.

# mango mousse rolls
## with lime gloss

This delightful mousse responds beautifully to being encased in a delicate roll and slicked with a tangy lime gloss. Make the mousse an hour or so in advance, to allow it to set.

To make the mousse, peel the mangoes and place 300 g/11 oz of the flesh into a food processor, then add the mascarpone cheese and sugar and whiz until you have a smooth purée.

Place the gelatine leaves in a small bowl, cover with cold water and leave to soften for 5 minutes. Warm the lemon juice in a small bowl over a pan of simmering water and add the gelatine. Stir until it has completely dissolved and add it to the mango mixture. Whisk the egg whites until stiff, then fold carefully into the mango mixture. Set in the fridge for an hour.

When the mousse has set, fill the crêpes with the mango mousse and roll up.

For the lime gloss, place the water, sugar and lime juice in a small pan and heat until the sugar has dissolved. Bubble the mixture for 4–5 minutes until shiny and thickened. Cool.

For the mango sauce, liquidize the remaining mango flesh and sweeten to taste with a little caster sugar. Add a glug of Malibu if desired. Break the chocolate into a small bowl and melt over a pan of gently simmering water.

To serve, place 2 Mango Mousse Rolls on each plate. Drizzle with Lime Gloss and spoon a little mango sauce around. Dip the prongs of a fork into the melted chocolate and drizzle sparingly over the rolls. Garnish with fresh mint and serve immediately.

SERVES 4

8 Sweet Crêpes (see page 42)

### for the mousse

2 large, sweet, ripe mangoes
200 g/7 oz/scant 1 cup
  mascarpone cheese
75 g/3 oz/6 tbsp caster
  (superfine) sugar
2 leaves gelatine
2 tbsp lemon juice
2 egg whites

### for the gloss

150 ml/5 fl oz/²⁄₃ cup water
90 g/3½ oz/7 tbsp caster
  (superfine) sugar
zest and juice 2 limes

### for the sauce

caster (superfine) sugar to taste
Malibu liqueur (optional)
50 g/2 oz dark Belgian
  chocolate (optional) to drizzle

fresh mint to garnish

# spiced pear *cannelloni*
## with brandy sauce

Spicy pears, laced with rum and spiked with stem ginger, make a fabulous filling for rolls. Add a glug of brandy sauce and grill until bubbling.

SERVES 4

8 Sweet Crêpes (see page 42)

### for the filling

40 g/1½ oz/3 tbsp butter

1 kg/2¼ lb ripe but firm pears, peeled and cut into large dice

50 g/2 oz/¼ cup caster (superfine) sugar

1 tsp ground cinnamon

1 tsp ground star anise

2 tbsp brandy

50 g/2 oz sultanas

4 knobs preserved stem ginger, finely chopped

4 tbsp preserved stem ginger syrup

### for the sauce

150ml/5fl oz/⅔ cup double (heavy) cream

Small quantity of brandy

2 tbsp icing (confectioner's) sugar

### for the topping

2 tbsp muscovado sugar

50 g/2 oz/½ cup pecans, chopped

15 g/½ oz/1 tbsp butter to grease an ovenproof dish

crème fraîche to serve

Lightly brush an ovenproof dish with melted butter. To make the filling, melt the butter in a large heavy-based pan and sauté the pears until they begin to turn a golden brown. Add the sugar and spices and continue to cook until the pears are soft. Add the brandy and set it alight. When the flames have died down, add the sultanas, stem ginger and syrup. Fill the crêpes with this mixture and roll them up. Place them side by side in the prepared dish.

For the sauce, lightly whip the cream, brandy and icing sugar until it just begins to thicken. Pour this mixture along the centre of the crêpes. Sprinkle over the muscovado sugar and scatter with the chopped pecans. Grill until golden brown and bubbling.

Serve immediately with crème fraîche.

# raspberry roly-poly
## with orange muscat sabayon

This is posh roly-poly and custard – and it's gorgeous! The raspberries are fresh, the roly-poly is a golden crêpe and the custard is light sabayon. For a very special dessert, these are especially nice served on individual plates and glazed under a hot grill. But if you prefer you could pop them in a buttered ovenproof dish and grill them all together.

SERVES 4

8 Sweet Crêpes (see page 42)

### for the filling

675 g/1½ lb/4 cups fresh raspberries
50 g/2 oz/½ cup caster (superfine) sugar

### for the sabayon

4 egg yolks
50 g/2 oz/¼ cup caster (superfine) sugar
120 ml/4 fl oz/½ cup Orange Muscat
  dessert wine

To make the raspberry filling, place 250 g/9 oz/1½ cups raspberries into a blender or food processor and purée, then sieve to remove the seeds. Sweeten with the sugar (the exact amount needed will vary according to how ripe your fruit is). Fold the remaining raspberries into the purée. Fill the crêpes with the raspberry mixture and lay 2, side by side, on each of 4 heatproof dessert plates. Set aside.

For the sabayon, place the egg yolks, sugar and Orange Muscat wine in a large bowl over a pan of gently simmering water and whisk until very light and thick. If you've never made a sabayon, just remember when you are whisking the egg yolks that the bowl should never become so hot that you can't touch it: this signals that the mixture is overheating and you may end up with a bowl of sweet scrambled eggs! The whisk should leave ribbon trails in the mixture when lifted. This will probably take around 10 minutes or so. When the sabayon is ready, pour it over the raspberry rolls and grill for a minute or so, until the sabayon is a beautiful golden brown.

Serve immediately.

# index

## Acknowledgements

*Crepes, Wraps and Rolls* was written and produced at much the same time as my first book *Dips, Dollops and Drizzles* and so many of the same people mentioned in its pages should step forward and take a bow once more!

They are Colin and Vivien at Pavilion – thank you for believing in me enough to do it all again! Maxine, my patient and good-humoured editor, and the rest of the Pavilion team for continuing to do such a great job behind the scenes – and for remaining such a brilliant gang to work with!

Many, many thanks also to: Geraldene Holt, for her help in lighting the way whenever I found myself in the dark about something! To Linda Tubby for being such a gem. To Dee for the loan of her *Poffertjes* Pan and to Clare and Julian for flying one back from Holland especially for me! To all my tasters and testers, my wonderful parents and family and once again, those special guys at home.